Stella Addison

members of Club
Why each chosen.
Influence of Papers.

THE

SIR ROGER DE COVERLEY PAPERS

FROM THE SPECTATOR

WITH QUESTIONS AND SUGGESTIONS FOR STUDY BY

HOMER K. UNDERWOOD, A. M.

HEAD OF THE ENGLISH DEPARTMENT, B. M. C. DURFEE HIGH
SCHOOL, FALL RIVER, MASS.

NEW YORK ·:· CINCINNATI ·:· CHICAGO

AMERICAN BOOK COMPANY

INTRODUCTION.

It is impossible to get an adequate idea of the "Spectator" without some knowledge of the "Tatler," of which it was the direct outcome. English newspapers had been for many years under government control, and gave only such news as the government allowed. The "Tatler" was a London newspaper founded by Richard Steele, and issued three times a week. It was designed to form and direct public opinion. Its price was one penny. Steele said its name was chosen in honor of the fair sex. The papers were signed "Isaac Bickerstaff, Esq.,"—a name borrowed from one of Swift's characters. The first number was issued April 12, 1709. The news was grouped under the titles of the different public assembly houses, where the men of that day met to discuss and gossip over current topics of state, literature, and society, much as they do in the social club-houses to-day. Thus, under the title "White's Chocolate House" was grouped the news of pleasure and entertainment; "Will's Coffee House," that of poetry and the drama; the "Grecian," learning; "St. James's," domestic topics, etc. The paper began by merely reporting the actions of men, but soon assumed the right to discuss the propriety of such actions. In the fifth number of the "Tatler" Addison discovered the identity of "Mr. Bickerstaff;" and he soon became one of the regular contributors, his first paper being No. 18. Addison and Steele had been friends from boy-hood, having attended Charterhouse School together, and after-wards Oxford. In the "Tatler" the essay soon took the place of that which was strictly news.

For the "Tatler" Steele wrote one hundred and eighty-eight papers, and Addison forty-two. There were two hundred and seventy-one in all. The "Tatler" attacked the immorality of the stage, gambling, dueling, and other public evils. It was dis-continued on Jan. 2, 1711. As Steele was a Whig, and accepted office under a Tory ministry, he thought it inconsistent to con-tinue a Whig paper, which, because of its sentiments, might cost him his place in the government. The "Spectator" was started two months after the discontinuance of the "Tatler;" viz., March 1, 1711. It was a daily, and ran as such for five hundred and fifty-five numbers, to Dec. 6, 1712. Its circulation was from three thousand to twenty thousand daily. For an interim of eighteen months it was discontinued. It then appeared three times a week, and died Dec. 20, 1714.

The "Tatler" was essentially a newspaper. The "Spectator" was meant particularly for those who had leisure to read, and were themselves thinkers. In place of the coffee and chocolate houses, and "Mr. Bickerstaff," was "The Spectator" and mem-bers of a "Club," including the following characters and types representing different qualities. Sir Roger de Coverley stood for simplicity and a high sense of honor; he was full of reminiscences of the past, while his character represented a country gentleman of the best kind. Sir Andrew Freeport was the enterprising, hard-headed, and hard-hearted money-maker. Captain Sentry represented the army and all its interests; the Templar, the world of taste and learning; the Clergyman, theology and philosophy; and Will Honeycomb was the elderly man of fashion, and the man about town.

(The chief object of the "Spectator" was to establish a rational standard of conduct in morals, manners, art, and literature.) It abstained from politics, and consisted of essays on the model gradually reached in the "Tatler." Of the six hundred and thirty-five papers contributed to the "Spectator," Addison wrote two hundred and seventy-four; Steele, two hundred and forty; Budgell, thirty-seven; Hughes, eleven; Grove, four; unknown writers, sixty-nine.

Dr. Johnson said, "Of the half not written by Addison, not half was good;" and that "whoever wishes to attain an English style familiar but not coarse, elegant but not ostentatious, must give his days and nights to the volumes of Addison."

The stamp of Addison is distinctly seen on the "Spectator," as that of Steele is upon the "Tatler." He once wrote that he wished it said of him when he died, that "he had brought philosophy out of closets and libraries, schools and colleges, to dwell in clubs and assemblies, at tea-tables and coffee-houses." He grasped the idea of making knowledge popular, and both Steele and he are said to have opened a new world to women. Conduct was the very groundwork of the essays.

It is said that the literary model adopted by Addison was taken from a distinguished Frenchman, La Bruyère, but that in his "Characters," La Bruyère described only what he saw, while Mr. Addison added to this the moral earnestness of a reformer. The papers comprising the "Spectator" must always maintain a high position in English literature, because of their quaintness of conceit, delicacy of touch, and purity of style and language. No careful student of our literature can afford to omit a conscien-

tious study of these specimens of English style. Among the
choicest essays of the "Spectator" are the thirty-three papers
comprising the "De Coverley" series. Of these, Addison wrote
twenty-one; Steele, nine; and Eustace Budgell, three.

Addison signed all that he wrote by the letters "C.," "L.," "I.,"
or "O." Steele usually signed his papers "R." or "T.;" and
Budgell, "X."

The chief events in Addison's life are briefly noted as follows.
He was born May 1, 1672, at his father's rectory, near Ames-
bury, Wiltshire, England. In 1683 his father became dean of
Lichfield, where young Addison attended school, soon changing
for the famous Charterhouse School in London, where he first
met his friend Richard Steele. In 1687 he entered Queen's
College, Oxford, where he early distinguished himself writing
Latin verses. He took the degree of M.A. in 1693, and a fel-
lowship in 1698, at Magdalen College. His Latin scholarship
soon gave him prominence in London, for he had in 1693 written a "Poetical Address praising Dryden's Translations," which
soon brought him to the attention of that poet. Montagu,
through Lord Somers, secured a pension for him of three hundred pounds in recognition of his literary services. He was expected to qualify for diplomatic services thereby. After traveling on the Continent for several years, he returned to England in
1703, and joined the famous Kitcat Club. In 1704 he was
appointed commissioner of appeals, succeeding John Locke, and
secured at the same time further prominence by writing a poem
celebrating the victory at Blenheim, called "The Campaign."
Later in the year he was appointed undersecretary of state.

In 1705 he published "Remarks on Several Parts of Italy,"

and in 1706 he was appointed undersecretary to Sir Charles Hedges. Lord Halifax, in 1707, paid a complimentary visit to the Elector of Hanover, and Addison accompanied him. This year he wrote the opera of "Rosamond," and a book called "The Present State of the War." He was elected to Parliament in 1708; but, the election being set aside, he was reëlected shortly after, standing for Malmesbury, and held his seat for life.

In 1711, at the age of thirty-nine, we find him alert, polished, cultivated, full of experience, ready for the work which was to give him lasting fame, — his contributions to the "Spectator." Besides the "De Coverley Papers," he wrote many others, humorous, critical, and serious, and seemed to put his most intense efforts and life into his contributions. His most important critical papers were those on "Paradise Lost," seventeen in number, published in the "Spectator" during 1712. His serious contributions were published in 1711, and included some exquisite hymns, the most familiar of which is "When all thy mercies, O my God." In 1713 he wrote the tragedy of "Cato," which had a long run at Drury Lane Theater. It was quickly translated into French, Italian, German, and Latin. After the death of the "Spectator," Steele established the "Guardian," to which Addison contributed fifty-one papers in 1713.

In 1714 Queen Anne died; and the Whigs were again restored to power, and Addison to politics. He was appointed to several important secretaryships, and became one of the lords commissioners of trade. In 1715 he published the "Freeholder," to which he contributed fifty-five papers. On Aug. 3, 1716, he was married to the Countess of Warwick, and the next year was appointed secretary of state in Sunderland's ministry. In consequence of ill health he resigned his position in 1718.

He died of dropsy and asthma, June 17, 1719, and is said to have sent for his stepson Warwick, and said to him, "See in what peace a Christian can die."

Richard Steele was born in Dublin, March 12, 1672, — the same year as Addison. His father was a lawyer. At twelve Steele entered Charterhouse School, and in 1690 entered Christ Church, Oxford. The next year he became postmaster at Merton College. Not long after, he entered the army as a cadet. The death of Queen Mary furnished him with material for a poem, which he published in 1695 under the title of "The Procession." While still in the army, he published the "Christian Hero," and a comedy, — the "Funeral," acted at Drury Lane, 1701. During the three following years he wrote several successful plays. In May, 1707, he was appointed gazetteer and gentleman in waiting to Prince George of Denmark. The same year he married Miss Mary Scurlock, a Welsh lady.

The "Tatler" was published in 1709, Steele the next year being made commissioner of stamps, and also losing his appointment as gazetteer. In 1711 the "Spectator" occupied most of his attention, while on March 12, 1713, he commenced the "Guardian," which ran a hundred and seventy-five numbers. The same year he both entered Parliament, and started the "Englishman." The year 1714 saw many contributions from his pen, largely critical and political.

He was expelled from the House of Commons in March, appointed surveyor of the royal stables at Hampton Court, deputy-lieutenant of the County of Middlesex, and supervisor of the Theater Royal. He became, in 1715, patentee of Drury Lane Theater, was knighted by George I., elected member of

Parliament for Boroughbridge, Yorkshire, published "An Account of the State of the Roman-Catholick Religion throughout the World," and began "Town Talk." He was appointed commissioner for forfeited estates in Scotland in 1716.

During 1719 the "Plebeian" was begun, as well as "The Spinster." Steele was again elected to Parliament in 1722, for Wendover, Bucks, and produced at Drury Lane, Nov. 7, "Conscious Lovers." He died Sept. 1, 1729, at Carmarthen, and is buried in St. Peter's Church there.

In addition to those mentioned above, Steele started five other papers, which had more or less success; namely, the "Englishman," "The Lover," "Tea-Table," "Chit Chat," the "Theater." An eminent English critic has said of him, "As a prose writer, Steele does not rank with the great masters of English style. He claimed, indeed, in his capacity as a Tatler, to use 'common speech,' to be even 'incorrect' if need be; and, it may be added, he sometimes abused this license, writing hastily and under pressure. His language is frequently involved and careless; and it is only when he is strongly stirred by his subject that he attains to real elevation and dignity of diction."

Eustace Budgell was born in the year 1685. His father was Gilbert Budgell of St. Thomas, Exeter. He was a cousin of Addison, and owes what small literary reputation he has to this fact. He entered Oxford in 1705 at Trinity College, and afterwards entered the Inner Temple. He was called to the bar, but his intimacy with Addison diverted him from his profession. His contributions to the "Spectator" were thirty-seven in number, mostly imitations of Addison's style.

In 1714 he published a translation of "Theophrastus." He

became in this year a member of the Irish House of Commons.
Through Addison's influence he became accountant-general in
1717, at a salary of four hundred pounds, which he lost in South
Sea speculations.   Many political pamphlets are attributed to
him. He contributed to the " Bee," the " Craftsman," and other
papers, the former being started by him.   In 1732 he published
" Memorials of the Life and Character of the Late Earl of Orrery
and the Family of Boyles."   He committed suicide in 1736, after having ruined his character by improper money transactions.
He is said to have been of unsound mind during the latter part
of his life.

CONTENTS

		PAGE
THE SPECTATOR	ADDISON	13
THE SPECTATOR CLUB	STEELE	18
SIR ROGER ON MEN OF FINE PARTS	STEELE	25
SIR ROGER AT HOME	ADDISON	29
SIR ROGER'S SERVANTS	STEELE	32
SIR ROGER AND WILL WIMBLE	ADDISON	36
SIR ROGER'S ANCESTORS	STEELE	39
NIGHT FEARS AT COVERLEY	ADDISON	43
A SUNDAY WITH SIR ROGER	ADDISON	47
SIR ROGER IN LOVE	STEELE	50
SIR ROGER'S ECONOMY	STEELE	56
BODILY EXERCISE	ADDISON	60
SIR ROGER AND THE CHASE	BUDGELL	64
MOLL WHITE, THE WITCH	ADDISON	69
LOVE-MAKING AT COVERLEY	STEELE	73
COUNTRY MANNERS	ADDISON	77
SIR ROGER'S POULTRY	ADDISON	80
THE ADAPTATION OF ANIMALS	ADDISON	84

PAGE

SIR ROGER AMONG HIS NEIGHBORS . . ADDISON 89

THE STORY OF FLORIO AND LEONILLA . . ADDISON 93

PARTY SPIRIT . . . . . . ADDISON 98

POLITICAL DISSENSIONS . . . . . ADDISON 102

SIR ROGER AND THE GYPSIES . . . ADDISON 106

THE SPECTATOR SUMMONED TO LONDON . ADDISON 109

THE JOURNEY TO LONDON . . . . STEELE 112

A DEBATE AT THE CLUB . . . . . STEELE 116

SIR ROGER IN LONDON . . . . ADDISON 120

SIR ROGER IN WESTMINSTER ABBEY . . ADDISON 125

SIR ROGER AND BEARDS . . . . BUDGELL 130

SIR ROGER AT THE PLAY . . . . . ADDISON 134

WILL HONEYCOMB AT THE CLUB . . BUDGELL 139

SIR ROGER AT SPRING GARDEN . . . ADDISON 142

SIR ROGER'S DEATH . . . . . ADDISON 146

SIR ROGER DE COVERLEY PAPERS.

THE SPECTATOR.

[*ADDISON*, in *SPECTATOR*, No. *1*.   *Thursday, March 1, 1710-11.*[1]]

*"Non fumum ex fulgore, sed ex fumo dare lucem
Cogitat, ut speciosa dehinc miracula promat."* [2]
HORACE, Ars Poetica, ver. 143.

I HAVE observed, that a reader seldom peruses a book with pleasure till he knows whether the writer of it be a black or a fair man, of a mild or choleric disposition, married or a bachelor, with other particulars of the like nature, that conduce very much to the right understanding of an author.   To gratify this curiosity, which is so natural to a reader, I design this paper, and my next, as prefatory discourses to my following writings, and shall give some account in them of the several persons that are engaged in this work.   As the chief trouble of compiling, digesting, and correcting will fall to my share, I must do myself the justice to open the work with my own history.

I was born to a small hereditary estate, which, according to the tradition of the village where it lies, was bounded by the

---

[1] Before 1752, when the Gregorian Calendar was adopted in England, it was customary to give two numbers for the year between the dates Jan. 1 and March 25 ; for the legal year began on the later date, while popularly the year was reckoned from the former.

[2] Roscommon's translation : —

"One with a flash begins, and ends in smoke;
Another out of smoke brings glorious light,
And (without raising expectation high)
Surprises us with dazzling miracles."

same hedges and ditches in William the Conqueror's[1] time that it is at present, and has been delivered down from father to son whole and entire, without the loss or acquisition of a single field or meadow, during the space of six hundred years. There runs a story in the family, that my mother dreamt that she had brought forth a judge. Whether this might proceed from a lawsuit which was then depending in the family, or my father's being a justice of the peace, I cannot determine; for I am not so vain as to think it presaged any dignity that I should arrive at in my future life, though that was the interpretation which the neighborhood put upon it. The gravity of my behavior at my very first appearance in the world seemed to favor my mother's dream: for, as she has often told me, I threw away my rattle before I was two months old, and would not make use of my coral till they had taken away the bells from it.

As for the rest of my infancy, there being nothing in it remarkable, I shall pass it over in silence. I find that, during my nonage, I had the reputation of a very sullen youth, but was always a favorite of my schoolmaster, who used to say, that my parts were solid, and would wear well. I had not been long at the university, before I distinguished myself by a most profound silence: for, during the space of eight years, excepting in the public exercises of the college, I scarce uttered the quantity of a hundred words; and indeed do not remember that I ever spoke three sentences together in my whole life. Whilst I was in this learned body, I applied myself with so much diligence to my studies, that there are very few celebrated books, either in the learned or the modern tongues, which I am not acquainted with.

Upon the death of my father I was resolved to travel into foreign countries, and therefore left the university, with the character of an odd unaccountable fellow, that had a great deal of learning, if I would but show it. An insatiable thirst after

---

[1] William, Duke of Normandy 1025–87, defeated King Harold at the battle of Hastings in 1066, and conquered England.

knowledge carried me into all the countries of Europe, in which there was anything new or strange to be seen; nay, to such a degree was my curiosity raised, that having read the controversies of some great men concerning the antiquities of Egypt, I made a voyage to Grand Cairo,[1] on purpose to take the measure of a pyramid; and, as soon as I had set myself right in that particular, returned to my native country with great satisfaction.

I have passed my latter years in this city, where I am frequently seen in most public places, though there are not above half a dozen of my select friends that know me; of whom my next paper shall give a more particular account. There is no place of general resort wherein I do not often make my appearance; sometimes I am seen thrusting my head into a round of politicians at Will's,[2] and listening with great attention to the narratives that are made in those little circular audiences. Sometimes I smoke a pipe at Child's;[2] and, while I seem attentive to

[1] This was probably a sarcasm on John Greaves, who published a book in 1646 entitled Pyramidographia, or a Description of the Pyramids in Egypt.

[2] The coffee and chocolate houses of the time of Addison were the chief places of resort. One asked in those days, not where men lived, but which was their coffee-house. They served instead of newspapers, and were arenas for public discussion, while each had its political or literary following. They were much more powerful in their day than any club of to-day. *Will's Coffee House* was at No. 1 Bow Street, Covent Garden, on the west side, corner of Russell Street, and was named from the original owner, William Urwin. Here the most intellectual men of the period gathered. In the Tatler it was made the center for poetry. *Child's* was located in St. Paul's Churchyard, where scientific people congregated particularly. *St. James's* was the last but one on the southwest corner of St. James Street, and was the headquarters for the Whigs during the reign of Queen Anne, and until the reign of George III. Addison, Steele, Swift, and later Goldsmith and Garrick, were among the distinguished frequenters of it. It is often mentioned in the Spectator. The *Grecian* was in Devereux Court, Strand. It was named after a Greek, Constantine, who originally kept it. It was the special resort of learned men and antiquarians. The *Cocoa Tree* was situated at 64 St. James Street. It once stood in Pall Mall. It was the Tory headquarters during Queen Anne's

nothing but the " Postman," [1] overhear the conversation of every
table in the room. I appear on Sunday nights at St. James's
Coffee House,[2] and sometimes join the little committee of politics
in the inner room, as one who comes there to hear and improve.
My face is likewise very well known at the Grecian,[2] the Cocoa Tree,[2] and in the theaters both of Drury Lane[3] and the Haymarket.[4] I have been taken for a merchant upon the Exchange
for above these ten years, and sometimes pass for a Jew in the
assembly of stockjobbers at Jonathan's.[2] In short, wherever I
see a cluster of people, I always mix with them, though I never
open my lips but in my own club.

Thus I live in the world, rather as a spectator of mankind, than
as one of the species; by which means I have made myself a
speculative statesman, soldier, merchant, and artisan, without
ever meddling with any practical part in life. I am very well
versed in the theory of a husband or a father, and can discern
the errors in the economy, business, and diversion of others, better than those who are engaged in them; as standers-by discover
blots, which are apt to escape those who are in the game. I
never espoused any party with violence, and am resolved to observe an exact neutrality between the Whigs and Tories,[5] unless

time. During the Stuart rebellion, in 1745, it was frequented largely by
Jacobites. *Jonathan's* was located on 'Change Alley, Cornhill, and was a
resort of stockjobbers and moneyed men.

[1] The favorite newspaper of the time, published weekly by a French
Protestant, M. Fonvive.   [2] See Note 2, p. 15.

[3] Perhaps the most famous theater in London. It was situated in Drury
Lane. No less than four different theaters have been built on the original
site, — the first in 1662; the second in 1674, by Sir Christopher Wren; the
third in 1794; the fourth in 1812. Many of the most famous plays and
actors made their first appearance there.

[4] The Haymarket, another famous London theater, was situated in the
Haymarket. It was known under different names; such as, the " Queen's
Theater," " King's," " Her Majesty's." It was first built and established by
Sir John Vanbrugh in 1703, and was burnt and rebuilt several times. The
present structure dates from 1869.

[5] The Whigs composed one of the two leading political parties in England.

I shall be forced to declare myself by the hostilities of either side. In short, I have acted in all the parts of my life as a looker-on, which is the character I intend to preserve in this paper.

I have given the reader just so much of my history and character, as to let him see I am not altogether unqualified for the business I have undertaken. As for other particulars in my life and adventures, I shall insert them in following papers, as I shall see occasion. In the mean time, when I consider how much I have seen, read, and heard, I begin to blame my own taciturnity; and since I have neither time nor inclination to communicate the fullness of my heart in speech, I am resolved to do it in writing; and to print myself out, if possible, before I die. I have been often told by my friends that it is pity so many useful discoveries which I have made, should be in the possession of a silent man. For this reason therefore, I shall publish a sheet full of thoughts every morning, for the benefit of my contemporaries; and if I can any way contribute to the diversion or improvement of the country in which I live, I shall leave it, when I am summoned out of it, with the secret satisfaction of thinking that I have not lived in vain.

There are three very material points which I have not spoken to in this paper, and which, for several important reasons, I must keep to myself, at least for some time: I mean, an account of my name, my age, and my lodgings. I must confess I would gratify my reader in anything that is reasonable; but as for these three particulars, though I am sensible they might tend very much to the embellishment of my paper, I cannot yet come to a resolution of communicating them to the public. They would indeed draw me out of that obscurity which I have enjoyed for many years, and expose me in public places to several salutes

In the reign of Charles II. the name "Whig" was a term of reproach given by the court party to their antagonists for holding the principles of the "Whigs," or fanatical Covenanters in Scotland. The name of "Tory" was given to the court party founded in 1653.

and civilities, which have been always very disagreeable to me; for the greatest pain I can suffer, is the being talked to, and being stared at. It is for this reason likewise, that I keep my complexion and dress, as very great secrets; though it is not impossible, but I may make discoveries of both in the progress of the work I have undertaken.

After having been thus particular upon myself, I shall in to-morrow's paper give an account of those gentlemen who are concerned with me in this work. For, as I have before intimated, a plan of it is laid and concerted (as all other matters of importance are) in a club. However, as my friends have engaged me to stand in the front, those who have a mind to correspond with me, may direct their letters to the "Spectator," at Mr. Buckley's,[1] in Little Britain. For I must further acquaint the reader, that though our Club meets only on Tuesdays and Thursdays, we have appointed a committee to sit every night, for the inspection of all such papers as may contribute to the advancement of the public weal.   C.

THE SPECTATOR CLUB.

[*STEELE, in SPECTATOR, No. 2.   Friday, March 2, 1710-11.*]

"Ast alii sex
Et plures uno conclamant ore." [2]
JUVENAL, Sat. vii. 167.

THE first of our society is a gentleman of Worcestershire,[3] of ancient descent, a baronet, his name Sir Roger de Coverley. His great-grandfather was inventor of that famous country-dance which is called after him. All who know that shire are very

---

[1] Samuel Buckley was the first publisher of the Spectator. His place was at the Dolphin, Little Britain Street. This street was for many years a center for the publishing trade.

[2] " Six more at least join their consenting voice."

[3] One of the principal western counties of England.

well acquainted with the parts and merits of Sir Roger. He is a gentleman that is very singular in his behavior, but his singularities proceed from his good sense, and are contradictions to the manners of the world, only as he thinks the world is in the wrong. However, this humor creates him no enemies, for he does nothing with sourness or obstinacy; and his being unconfined to modes and forms, makes him but the readier and more capable to please and oblige all who know him. When he is in town he lives in Soho Square:[1] it is said, he keeps himself a bachelor by reason he was crossed in love by a perverse beautiful widow of the next county to him. Before this disappointment, Sir Roger was what you call a fine gentleman, had often supped with my Lord Rochester and Sir George Etherege,[2] fought a duel upon his first coming to town, and kicked Bully Dawson[3] in a public coffee-house for calling him youngster. But being ill used by the above-mentioned widow, he was very serious for a year and a half; and though his temper being naturally jovial, he at last got over it, he grew careless of himself and never dressed afterwards; he continues to wear a coat and doublet of the same cut that were in fashion at the time of his repulse, which, in his merry humors, he tells us, has been in and out twelve times since he first wore it. He is now in his fifty-sixth year, cheerful, gay, and hearty, keeps a good house in both town and country; a great lover of mankind; but there is such a mirthful caste in his behavior, that he is rather beloved than esteemed. His tenants grow rich, his servants look satisfied, all the young women profess love to him, and the young men are glad of his company: when he comes into a house he calls the servants by their names, and talks all

---

[1] A square in London, on the south side of Oxford Street. Its name is derived from an old cry used in hunting, when the hare was found. Until about sixty years ago it was a center of fashion. It was built in 1681.

[2] Lord Rochester and Sir George Etherege were noted wits and writers during the reign of Charles II.

[3] Bully Dawson was a noted London sharper and swaggerer during the reign of Charles II.

the way upstairs to a visit. I must not omit that Sir Roger is a
justice of the quorum;[1] that he fills the chair at a quarter-session
with great abilities, and three months ago, gained universal applause by explaining a passage in the game-act.

The gentleman next in esteem and authority among us, is
another bachelor, who is a member of the Inner Temple;[2] a
man of great probity, wit, and understanding; but he has chosen
his place of residence rather to obey the direction of an old hu-
morsome father, than in pursuit of his own inclinations. He was
placed there to study the laws of the land, and is the most learned
of any of the house in those of the stage. Aristotle and Longinus[3] are much better understood by him than Littleton or
Cooke.[4] The father sends up every post questions relating to
marriage-articles, leases, and tenures, in the neighborhood; all
which questions he agrees with an attorney to answer and take
care of in the lump. He is studying the passions themselves,
when he should be inquiring into the debates among men which
arise from them. He knows the argument of each of the ora-
tions of Demosthenes and Tully,[5] but not one case in the reports
of our own courts. No one ever took him for a fool, but none,
except his intimate friends, know he has a great deal of wit. This
turn makes him at once both disinterested and agreeable: as few

[1] A distinction conferred upon certain justices of the peace in England, by
directing that they must be among those holding quarter-sessions or the
quarterly sessions of court in the county.

[2] One of the four societies of students and practicers of the law of England; also the name of one of the buildings where law students and barristers
have their chambers. Others are the Middle Temple, Lincoln's Inn, and
Gray's Inn.

[3] Aristotle and Longinus were celebrated Greek philosophers. Aristotle
lived in the third century before, and Longinus in the third century after,
Christ.

[4] Littleton and Cooke (more commonly written Coke or Cook) were noted
English jurists and annotators of the fifteenth and sixteenth centuries re-
spectively. They were the great authorities on land tenures.

[5] Demosthenes (385–322 B.C.) was the greatest Greek orator; and Mar-
cus Tullius (Tully) Cicero (106–43 B.C.), the greatest Roman orator.

of his thoughts are drawn from business, they are most of them fit for conversation. His taste of books is a little too just for the age he lives in; he has read all, but approves of very few. His familiarity with the customs, manners, actions, and writings of the ancients, makes him a very delicate observer of what occurs to him in the present world. He is an excellent critic, and the time of the play is his hour of business; exactly at five he passes through New Inn,[1] crosses through Russell Court;[2] and takes a turn at Will's till the play begins; he has his shoes rubbed and his periwig powdered at the barber's as you go into the Rose.[3] It is for the good of the audience when he is at a play, for the actors have an ambition to please him.

The person of next consideration is Sir Andrew Freeport, a merchant of great eminence in the city of London: a person of indefatigable industry, strong reason, and great experience. His notions of trade are noble and generous, and (as every rich man has usually some sly way of jesting, which would make no great figure were he not a rich man) he calls the sea the British Common. He is acquainted with commerce in all its parts, and will tell you that it is a stupid and barbarous way to extend dominion by arms; for true power is to be got by arts and industry. He will often argue, that if this part of our trade were well cultivated, we should gain from one nation; and if another, from another. I have heard him prove that diligence makes more lasting acquisitions than valor, and that sloth has ruined more nations than the sword. He abounds in several frugal maxims, amongst which the greatest favorite is, "A penny saved is a penny got." A general trader of good sense is pleasanter company than a general scholar; and Sir Andrew having a natural unaffected

---

[1] A building where law students and barristers had their chambers.

[2] This was a narrow passage, for foot-passengers only, leading from Drury Lane into Catherine Street, Covent Garden.

[3] A noted tavern in London. It stood in Russell Street, Covent Garden, adjoining Drury Lane Theater. It was a famous resort during Queen Anne's reign.

eloquence, the perspicuity of his discourse gives the same pleasure that wit would in another man.   He has made his fortunes
himself ; and says that England may be richer than other king-
doms, by as plain methods as he himself is richer than other men ;
though at the same time I can say this of him, that there is not a
point in the compass, but blows home a ship in which he is an
owner.

Next to Sir Andrew in the club-room sits Captain Sentry, a
gentleman of great courage, good understanding, but invincible
modesty.   He is one of those that deserve very well, but are very
awkward at putting their talents within the observation of such
as should take notice of them.   He was some years a captain,
and behaved himself with great gallantry in several engagements,
and at several sieges ; but having a small estate of his own, and
being next heir to Sir Roger, he has quitted a way of life in
which no man can rise suitably to his merit, who is not something of a courtier, as well as a soldier.   I have heard him often
lament, that in a profession where merit is placed in so conspicuous a view, impudence should get the better of modesty.   When
he has talked to this purpose, I never heard him make a sour
expression, but frankly confess that he left the world, because he
was not fit for it.   A strict honesty and an even regular behavior, are in themselves obstacles to him that must press through
crowds who endeavor at the same end with himself, the favor of
a commander.   He will, however, in this way of talk, excuse
generals, for not disposing according to men's desert, or inquiring
into it : for, says he, that great man who has a mind to help me,
has as many to break through to come at me, as I have to come
at him : therefore he will conclude, that the man who would
make a figure, especially in a military way, must get over all false
modesty, and assist his patron against the importunity of other
pretenders, by a proper assurance in his own vindication.   He
says it is a civil cowardice to be backward in asserting what you
ought to expect, as it is a military fear to be slow in attacking
when it is your duty.   With this candor does the gentleman speak

of himself and others. The same frankness runs through all his conversation. The military part of his life has furnished him with many adventures, in the relation of which he is very agreeable to the company; for he is never overbearing, though accustomed to command men in the utmost degree below him; nor ever too obsequious, from a habit of obeying men highly above him.

But that our society may not appear a set of humorists unacquainted with the gallantries and pleasures of the age, we have among us the gallant Will Honeycomb, a gentleman who, according to his years, should be in the decline of his life, but having ever been very careful of his person, and always had a very easy fortune, time has made but very little impression, either by wrinkles on his forehead, or traces in his brain. His person is well turned, and of a good height. He is very ready at that sort of discourse with which men usually entertain women. He has all his life dressed very well, and remembers habits as others do men. He can smile when one speaks to him, and laughs easily. He knows the history of every mode, and can inform you from which of the French king's wenches our wives and daughters had this manner of curling their hair, that way of placing their hoods; whose vanity to show her foot made the petticoat so short in such a year. In a word, all his conversation and knowledge has been in the female world: as other men of his age will take notice to you what such a minister said upon such and such an occasion, he will tell you when the Duke of Monmouth[1] danced at court such a woman was then smitten, another was taken with him at the head of his troop in the Park. In all these important relations, he has ever about the same time received a kind glance, or a blow of a fan, from some celebrated beauty, mother of the

---

[1] James Scott, Duke of Monmouth, was a son of Charles II., and born in 1649. He was also created Duke of Buccleuch. As heir to the throne, and an ardent Protestant, he invaded England in 1685, and gained a victory at Axminster. He was afterwards defeated by James II., at the battle of Sedgemoor, and executed July, 1685.

present Lord Such-a-one. If you speak of a young Commoner that said a lively thing in the House, he starts up, " He has good blood in his veins, Tom Mirabell begot him, the rogue cheated me in that affair ; that young fellow's mother used me more like a dog than any woman I ever made advances to." This way of talking of his, very much enlivens the conversation among us of a more sedate turn ; and I find there is not one of the company but myself, who rarely speak at all, but speaks of him as of that sort of man, who is usually called a well-bred fine gentleman. To conclude his character, where women are not concerned, he is an honest worthy man.

I cannot tell whether I am to account him whom I am next to speak of, as one of our company ; for he visits us but seldom, but when he does, it adds to every man else a new enjoyment of himself. He is a clergyman, a very philosophic man, of general learning, great sanctity of life, and the most exact good breeding. He has the misfortune to be of a very weak constitution, and consequently cannot accept of such cares and business as preferments in his function would oblige him to : he is therefore among divines what a chamber-counselor is among lawyers. The probity of his mind, and the integrity of his life, create him followers, as being eloquent or loud advances others. He seldom introduces the subject he speaks upon ; but we are so far gone in years, that he observes when he is among us, an earnestness to have him fall on some divine topic, which he always treats with much authority, as one who has no interests in this world, as one who is hastening to the object of all his wishes, and conceives hope from his decays and infirmities. These are my ordinary companions. R.

SIR ROGER ON MEN OF FINE PARTS.

[*STEELE, in* SPECTATOR, *No. 6. Wednesday, March 7, 1710-11.*]

" *Credebant hoc grande nefas, et morte piandum,*
  Si juvenis vetulo non assurrexerat." [1]

JUVENAL, Sat. xiii. 54.

I KNOW no evil under the sun so great as the abuse of the understanding, and yet there is no one vice more common. It has diffused itself through both sexes, and all qualities of mankind; and there is hardly that person to be found, who is not more concerned for the reputation of wit and sense, than honesty and virtue. But this unhappy affectation of being wise rather than honest, witty than good-natured, is the source of most of the ill habits of life. Such false impressions are owing to the abandoned writings of men of wit, and the awkward imitation of the rest of mankind.

For this reason, Sir Roger was saying last night, that he was of opinion that none but men of fine parts deserve to be hanged. The reflections of such men are so delicate upon all occurrences which they are concerned in, that they should be exposed to more than ordinary infamy and punishment, for offending against such quick admonitions as their own souls give them, and blunting the fine edge of their minds in such a manner, that they are no more shocked at vice and folly, than men of slower capacities. There is no greater monster in being, than a very ill man of great parts: he lives like a man in a palsy, with one side of him dead. While perhaps he enjoys the satisfaction of luxury, of wealth, of ambition, he has lost the taste of good will, of friendship, of innocence. Scarecrow, the beggar in Lincoln's Inn Fields,[2] who

---

[1] Free translation: —

    " 'Twas impious then (so much was age revered)
      For youth to keep their seats when an old man appeared."

[2] This was once an open space for public meetings. It derived its name from Henry de Lacy, Earl of Lincoln, who had a house erected there in the

disabled himself in his right leg, and asks alms all day to get himself a warm supper at night, is not half so despicable a wretch as such a man of sense. The beggar has no relish above sensations; he finds rest more agreeable than motion; and while he has a warm fire, never reflects that he deserves to be whipped. Every man who terminates his satisfaction and enjoyments within the supply of his own necessities and passions, is, says Sir Roger, in my eye as poor a rogue as Scarecrow. "But," continued he, "for the loss of public and private virtue we are beholden to your men of parts forsooth; it is with them no matter what is done, so it is done with an air. But to me who am so whimsical in a corrupt age as to act according to nature and reason, a selfish man in the most shining circumstance and equipage, appears in the same condition with the fellow above mentioned, but more contemptible in proportion to what more he robs the public of and enjoys above him. I lay it down therefore for a rule, that the whole man is to move together; that every action of any importance is to have a prospect of public good; and that the general tendency of our indifferent actions ought to be agreeable to the dictates of reason, of religion, of good breeding; without this, a man, as I have before hinted, is hopping instead of walking, he is not in his entire and proper motion."

While the honest knight was thus bewildering himself in good starts, I looked intentively upon him, which made him I thought collect his mind a little. "What I aim at," says he, "is, to represent, that I am of opinion, to polish our understandings and neglect our manners is of all things the most inexcusable. Reason should govern passion, but instead of that, you see, it is often subservient to it; and, as unaccountable as one would think it, a wise man is not always a good man." This degeneracy is not only the guilt of particular persons, but also at some times of a whole people; and perhaps it may appear upon examination, that the most polite ages are the least virtuous. This may be

reign of Edward I. It became an inn of court in 1310. The new buildings were opened in 1845. It is one of the most beautiful courts of London.

attributed to the folly of admitting wit and learning as merit in themselves, without considering the application of them. By this means it becomes a rule not so much to regard what we do, as how we do it. But this false beauty will not pass upon men of honest minds and true taste. Sir Richard Blackmore[1] says, with as much good sense as virtue, " It is a mighty dishonor and shame to employ excellent faculties and abundance of wit, to humor and please men in their vices and follies. The great enemy of mankind, notwithstanding his wit and angelic faculties, is the most odious being in the whole creation." He goes on soon after to say very generously, that he undertook the writing of his poem "to rescue the Muses out of the hands of ravishers, to restore them to their sweet and chaste mansions, and to engage them in an employment suitable to their dignity." This certainly ought to be the purpose of every man who appears in public; and whoever does not proceed upon that foundation, injures his country as fast as he succeeds in his studies. When modesty ceases to be the chief ornament of one sex, and integrity of the other, society is upon a wrong basis, and we shall be ever after without rules to guide our judgment in what is really becoming and ornamental. Nature and reason direct one thing, passion and humor another: to follow the dictates of the two latter, is going into a road that is both endless and intricate; when we pursue the other, our passage is delightful, and what we aim at easily attainable.

I do not doubt but England is at present as polite a nation as any in the world; but any man who thinks can easily see, that the affectation of being gay and in fashion has very near eaten up our good sense and our religion. Is there anything so just, as that mode and gallantry should be built upon exerting ourselves in what is proper and agreeable to the institutions of justice and piety among us? And yet is there anything more common, than that we run in perfect contradiction to them? All

[1] Sir Richard Blackmore (1650–1729) was an English writer and poet. His poem The Creation (1712) was much admired by Addison.

which is supported by no other pretension, than that it is done with what we call a good grace.

Nothing ought to be held laudable or becoming, but what nature itself should prompt us to think so. Respect to all kind of superiors is founded methinks upon instinct; and yet what is so ridiculous as age? I make this abrupt transition to the mention of this vice more than any other, in order to introduce a little story, which I think a pretty instance that the most polite age is in danger of being the most vicious.

"It happened at Athens, during a public representation of some play exhibited in honor of the commonwealth that an old gentleman came too late for a place suitable to his age and quality. Many of the young gentlemen who observed the difficulty and confusion he was in, made signs to him that they would accommodate him if he came where they sat: the good man bustled through the crowd accordingly; but when he came to the seats to which he was invited, the jest was to sit close, and expose him, as he stood out of countenance, to the whole audience. The frolic went round all the Athenian benches. But on those occasions there were also particular places assigned for foreigners: when the good man skulked towards the boxes appointed for the Lacedæmonians,[1] that honest people, more virtuous than polite, rose up all to a man, and with the greatest respect received him among them. The Athenians being suddenly touched with a sense of the Spartan virtue, and their own degeneracy, gave a thunder of applause; and the old man cried out, 'The Athenians understand what is good, but the Lacedæmonians practice it.'"   R.

---

[1] Lacedæmonians, or Spartans, were the people of a neighboring republic of Greece. They were brought up under a strict and peculiar code of laws, intended to inculcate, among other things, undaunted courage, fidelity to the state, and respect for the aged.

SIR ROGER AT HOME.

[*ADDISON*, in *SPECTATOR*, No. *106*. *Monday*, *July 2*, *1711*.]

"Hinc tibi copia
Manabit ad plenum, benigno
Ruris honorum opulenta cornu." [1]
HORACE, Lib. I., Ode xvii. 14.

HAVING often received an invitation from my friend Sir Roger de Coverley to pass away a month with him in the country, I last week accompanied him thither, and am settled with him for some time at his country house, where I intend to form several of my ensuing speculations. Sir Roger, who is very well acquainted with my humor, lets me rise and go to bed when I please, dine at his own table or in my chamber as I think fit, sit still and say nothing without bidding me be merry. When the gentlemen of the country come to see him, he only shows me at a distance: as I have been walking in his fields I have observed them stealing a sight of me over a hedge, and have heard the knight desiring them not to let me see them, for that I hated to be stared at.

I am the more at ease in Sir Roger's family, because it consists of sober and staid persons; for as the knight is the best master in the world, he seldom changes his servants; and as he is beloved by all about him, his servants never care for leaving him; by this means his domestics are all in years, and grown old with their master. You would take his valet de chambre for his brother, his butler is gray-headed, his groom is one of the gravest men that I have ever seen, and his coachman has the looks of a privy counselor. You see the goodness of the master even in the

[1] Free translation: —

" Here plenty's liberal horn shall pour
Of fruits for thee a copious shower,
Rich honors of the quiet plain."

old house-dog, and in a gray pad that is kept in the stable with great care and tenderness out of regard to his past services, though he has been useless for several years.

I could not but observe with a great deal of pleasure the joy that appeared in the countenances of these ancient domestics upon my friend's arrival at his country seat. Some of them could not refrain from tears at the sight of their old master; every one of them pressed forward to do something for him, and seemed discouraged if they were not employed. At the same time the good old knight, with a mixture of the father and the master of the family, tempered the inquiries after his own affairs with several kind questions relating to themselves. This humanity and good nature engages everybody to him, so that when he is pleasant upon any of them, all his family are in good humor, and none so much as the person whom he diverts himself with: on the contrary, if he coughs, or betrays any infirmity of old age, it is easy for a stander-by to observe a secret concern in the looks of all his servants.

My worthy friend has put me under the particular care of his butler, who is a very prudent man, and, as well as the rest of his fellow-servants, wonderfully desirous of pleasing me, because they have often heard their master talk of me as of his particular friend.

My chief companion, when Sir Roger is diverting himself in the woods or the fields, is a very venerable man who is ever with Sir Roger, and has lived at his house in the nature of a chaplain above thirty years. This gentleman is a person of good sense and some learning, of a very regular life and obliging conversation: he heartily loves Sir Roger, and knows that he is very much in the old knight's esteem, so that he lives in the family rather as a relation than a dependant.

I have observed in several of my papers, that my friend Sir Roger, amidst all his good qualities, is something of a humorist; and that his virtues, as well as imperfections, are as it were tinged by a certain extravagance, which makes them particularly his, and distinguishes them from those of other men. This cast of mind, as it is generally very innocent in itself, so it renders his conversation highly agreeable, and more delightful than the same degree of sense and virtue would appear in their common and ordinary colors. As I was walking with him last night, he asked me how I liked the good man whom I have just now mentioned? and without staying for my answer told me, that he was afraid of being insulted with Latin and Greek at his own table; for which reason he desired a particular friend of his at the university to find him out a clergyman rather of plain sense than much learning, of a good aspect, a clear voice, a sociable temper, and, if possible, a man that understood a little of backgammon. "My friend," says Sir Roger, "found me out this gentleman, who, besides the endowments required of him, is, they tell me, a good scholar, though he does not show it. I have given him the parsonage of the parish; and because I know his value have settled upon him a good annuity for life. If he outlives me, he shall find that he was higher in my esteem than perhaps he thinks he is. He has now been with me thirty years; and though he does not know I have taken notice of it, has never in all that time asked anything of me for himself, though he is every day soliciting me for something in behalf of one or other of my tenants his parishioners. There has not been a lawsuit in the parish since he has lived among them: if any dispute arises they apply themselves to him for the decision; if they do not acquiesce in his judgment, which I think never happened above once or twice at most, they appeal to me. At his first settling with me, I made him a present of all the good sermons which have been printed in English, and only begged of him that every Sunday he would pronounce one of them in the pulpit. Accordingly, he has digested them into such a series, that they follow one another naturally, and make a continued system of practical divinity."

As Sir Roger was going on in his story, the gentleman we were talking of came up to us; and upon the knight's asking him who preached to-morrow (for it was Saturday night) told us, the Bishop

of St. Asaph[1] in the morning, and Dr. South[2] in the afternoon.
He then showed us his list of preachers for the whole year, where
I saw with a great deal of pleasure Archbishop Tillotson,[2] Bishop
Saunderson,[2] Dr. Barrow,[2] Dr. Calamy,[2] with several living authors
who have published discourses of practical divinity.   I no sooner
saw this venerable man in the pulpit, but I very much approved
of my friend's insisting upon the qualifications of a good aspect
and a clear voice; for I was so charmed with the gracefulness
of his figure and delivery, as well as with the discourses he pro-
nounced, that I think I never passed any time more to my satisfaction.   A sermon repeated after this manner, is like the composition of a poet in the mouth of a graceful actor.

I could heartily wish that more of our country clergy would
follow this example; and instead of wasting their spirits in laborious compositions of their own, would endeavor after a handsome elocution, and all those other talents that are proper to en-
force what has been penned by greater masters.   This would not
only be more easy to themselves, but more edifying to the people.

L.

SIR ROGER'S SERVANTS.

[*STEELE, in SPECTATOR, No. 107.   Tuesday, July 3, 1711.*]

> "*Æsopo ingentem statuam posuere Attici,*
> *Servumque collocarunt æterna in basi,*
> *Patere honoris scirent ut cuncti viam.*"[3]
> PHÆDRUS, Ep. i. 2.

THE reception, manner of attendance, undisturbed freedom
and quiet, which I meet with here in the country, has confirmed me in the opinion I always had, that the general corrup-

---

[1] A bishopric of North Wales, founded by Kentigern, Bishop of Glasgow,
about 560.   William Fleetwood (1656–1723), afterwards Bishop of Ely, an
eloquent preacher and writer, is here referred to.

[2] South, Tillotson, Saunderson, Barrow, and Calamy were all celebrated
English divines of the seventeenth century.

[3] "The Athenians erected a large statue to Æsop, and placed him, though

tion of manners in servants is owing to the conduct of masters. The aspect of every one in the family carries so much satisfaction, that it appears he knows the happy lot which has befallen him in being a member of it. There is one particular which I have seldom seen but at Sir Roger's; it is usual in all other places, that servants fly from the parts of the house through which their master is passing; on the contrary, here they industriously place themselves in his way; and it is on both sides, as it were, understood as a visit, when the servants appear without calling. This proceeds from the humane and equal temper of the man of the house, who also perfectly well knows how to enjoy a great estate, with such economy as ever to be much beforehand. This makes his own mind untroubled, and consequently unapt to vent peevish expressions, or give passionate or inconsistent orders to those about him. Thus respect and love go together; and a certain cheerfulness in performance of their duty is the particular distinction of the lower part of this family. When a servant is called before his master, he does not come with an expectation to hear himself rated for some trivial fault, threatened to be stripped, or used with any other unbecoming language, which mean masters often give to worthy servants; but it is often to know, what road he took that he came so readily back according to order; whether he passed by such a ground, if the old man who rents it is in good health: or whether he gave Sir Roger's love to him, or the like.

A man who preserves a respect, founded on his benevolence to his dependants, lives rather like a prince than a master in his family; his orders are received as favors, rather than duties; and the distinction of approaching him is part of the reward for executing what is commanded by him.

There is another circumstance in which my friend excels in his management, which is the manner of rewarding his servants: he has ever been of opinion, that giving his cast clothes to be worn

a slave, on a lasting pedestal, to show that the way to honor lies indifferently to all."

by valets has a very ill effect upon little minds, and creates a silly sense of equality between the parties, in persons affected only with outward things. I have heard him often pleasant on this occasion, and describe a young gentleman abusing his man in that coat, which a month or two before was the most pleasing distinction he was conscious of in himself. He would turn his discourse still more pleasantly upon the ladies' bounties of this kind; and I have heard him say he knew a fine woman, who distributed rewards and punishments in giving becoming or unbecoming dresses to her maids.

But my good friend is above these little instances of good will, in bestowing only trifles on his servants; a good servant to him is sure of having it in his choice very soon of being no servant at all. As I before observed, he is so good a husband, and knows so thoroughly that the skill of the purse is the cardinal virtue of this life; I say, he knows so well that frugality is the support of generosity, that he can often spare a large fine when a tenement falls,[1] and give that settlement to a good servant who has a mind to go into the world, or make a stranger pay the fine to that servant, for his more comfortable maintenance, if he stays in his service.

A man of honor and generosity considers, it would be miserable to himself to have no will but that of another, though it were of the best person breathing, and for that reason goes on as fast as he is able to put his servants into independent livelihoods. The greatest part of Sir Roger's estate is tenanted by persons who have served himself or his ancestors. It was to me extremely pleasant to observe the visitants from several parts to welcome his arrival into the country: and all the difference that I could take notice of between the late servants who came to see

---

[1] In reference to this passage, the following quotation from Blackstone's Commentaries affords an adequate explanation: "A tenement falls, or *alienates*. A consequence of tenure by knight service was that of fines due the lord for every alienation, whenever the tenant had occasion to make over his land to another."

him, and those who staid in the family, was that these latter were looked upon as finer gentlemen and better courtiers.

This manumission and placing them in a way of livelihood, I look upon as only what is due to a good servant, which encouragement will make his successor be as diligent, as humble, and as ready as he was. There is something wonderful in the narrowness of those minds, which can be pleased, and be barren of bounty to those who please them.

One might, on this occasion, recount the sense that great persons in all ages have had of the merit of their dependants, and the heroic services which men have done their masters in the extremity of their fortunes; and shown to their undone patrons, that fortune was all the difference between them; but as I design this my speculation only as a gentle admonition to thankless masters, I shall not go out of the occurrences of common life, but assert it as a general observation, that I never saw, but in Sir Roger's family, and one or two more, good servants treated as they ought to be. Sir Roger's kindness extends to their children's children, and this very morning he sent his coachman's grandson to prentice.[1] I shall conclude this paper with an account of a picture in his gallery, where there are many which will deserve my future observation.

At the very upper end of this handsome structure I saw the portraiture of two young men standing in a river, the one naked, the other in a livery. The person supported seemed half dead, but still so much alive as to show in his face exquisite joy and love towards the other. I thought the fainting figure resembled my friend Sir Roger; and looking at the butler, who stood by me, for an account of it, he informed me that the person in the livery was a servant of Sir Roger's, who stood on the shore while his master was swimming, and observing him taken with some sudden illness, and sink under water, jumped in and saved him. He told me Sir Roger took off the dress he was in as soon as he came home, and by a great bounty at that time, followed by his

---

[1] An obsolete or colloquial form of "apprentice."

favor ever since, had made him master of that pretty seat which
we saw at a distance as we came to this house. I remembered
indeed Sir Roger said there lived a very worthy gentleman, to
whom he was highly obliged, without mentioning anything further. Upon my looking a little dissatisfied at some part of the
picture my attendant informed me that it was against Sir Roger's
will, and at the earnest request of the gentleman himself, that he
was drawn in the habit in which he had saved his master.

R.

SIR ROGER AND WILL WIMBLE.

[*ADDISON, in SPECTATOR, No. 108. Wednesday, July 4, 1711.*]

"*Gratis anhelans, multa agendo nihil agens.*" [1]
PHÆDRUS, Lib. II. Fab. v. 3.

AS I was yesterday morning walking with Sir Roger before
his house, a country fellow brought him a huge fish, which,
he told him, Mr. William Wimble had caught that very morning;
and that he presented it, with his service to him, and intended
to come and dine with him. At the same time he delivered a
letter, which my friend read to me as soon as the messenger left
him.

SIR ROGER,— I desire you to accept of a jack, which is the best I have
caught this season. I intend to come and stay with you a week, and see
how the perch bite in the Black River. I observed with some concern, the
last time I saw you upon the bowling-green, that your whip wanted a lash to
it; I will bring half a dozen with me that I twisted last week, which I hope
will serve you all the time you are in the country. I have not been out of
the saddle for six days last past, having been at Eton [2] with Sir John's eldest
son. He takes to his learning hugely. I am, sir,
Your humble servant,
WILL WIMBLE.

[1] " Out of breath to no purpose, and very busy about nothing."
[2] The most famous preparatory school in England, founded by Henry VI.
in 1440, in Buckinghamshire.

This extraordinary letter, and message that accompanied it, made me very curious to know the character and quality of the gentleman who sent them; which I found to be as follows. Will Wimble is younger brother to a baronet, and descended of the ancient family of the Wimbles. He is now between forty and fifty; but being bred to no business and born to no estate, he generally lives with his elder brother as superintendent of his game. He hunts a pack of dogs better than any man in the country, and is very famous for finding out a hare. He is extremely well versed in all the little handicrafts of an idle man: he makes a May-fly[1] to a miracle; and furnishes the whole country with angle-rods. As he is a good-natured officious fellow, and very much esteemed upon account of his family, he is a welcome guest at every house, and keeps up a good correspondence among all the gentlemen about him. He carries a tulip-root in his pocket from one to another, or exchanges a puppy between a couple of friends that live perhaps in the opposite sides of the county. Will is a particular favorite of all the young heirs, whom he frequently obliges with a net that he has weaved, or a setting-dog[2] that he has trained himself. These gentleman-like manufactures and obliging little humors, make Will the darling of the country.

Sir Roger was proceeding in the character of him, when we saw him make up to us with two or three hazel-twigs in his hand that he had cut in Sir Roger's woods, as he came through them, in his way to the house. I was very much pleased to observe on one side the hearty and sincere welcome with which Sir Roger received him, and on the other, the secret joy which his guest discovered at sight of the good old knight. After the first salutes were over, Will desired Sir Roger to lend him one of his servants to carry a set of shuttlecocks he had with him in a little box to a lady that lived about a mile off, to whom it seems he had promised such a present for above this half-year. Sir Roger's back was no sooner turned but honest Will began to tell me of a large

---

[1] A fishing-fly.　　　　　　　[2] A setter-dog.

cock-pheasant that he had sprung in one of the neighboring woods, with two or three other adventures of the same nature. Odd and uncommon characters are the game that I look for, and most delight in; for which reason I was as much pleased with the novelty of the person that talked to me, as he could be for his life with the springing of a pheasant, and therefore listened to him with more than ordinary attention.

In the midst of his discourse the bell rung to dinner, where the gentleman I have been speaking of had the pleasure of seeing the huge jack, he had caught, served up for the first dish in a most sumptuous manner. Upon our sitting down to it he gave us a long account how he had hooked it, played with it, foiled it, and at length drew it out upon the bank, with several other particulars that lasted all the first course. A dish of wild fowl that came afterwards furnished conversation for the rest of the dinner, which concluded with a late invention of Will's for improving the quail-pipe.[1]

Upon withdrawing into my room after dinner, I was secretly touched with compassion towards the honest gentleman that had dined with us; and could not but consider with a great deal of concern, how so good a heart and such busy hands were wholly employed in trifles; that so much humanity should be so little beneficial to others, and so much industry so little advantageous to himself. The same temper of mind and application to affairs might have recommended him to the public esteem, and have raised his fortune in another station of life. What good to his country or himself might not a trader or merchant have done with such useful though ordinary qualifications?

Will Wimble's is the case of many a younger brother of a great family, who had rather see their children starve like gentlemen, than thrive in a trade or profession that is beneath their quality. This humor fills several parts of Europe with pride and beggary. It is the happiness of a trading nation, like ours, that the younger sons, though incapable of any liberal art or profession, may be

---

[1] A call, or pipe, for alluring quail to a net.

placed in such a way of life, as may perhaps enable them to vie with the best of their family : accordingly we find several citizens that were launched into the world with narrow fortunes, rising by an honest industry to greater estates than those of their elder brothers. It is not improbable but Will was formerly tried at divinity, law, or physic ; and that finding his genius did not lie that way, his parents gave him up at length to his own inventions. But certainly, however improper he might have been for studies of a higher nature, he was perfectly well turned for the occupations of trade and commerce. As I think this is a point which cannot be too much inculcated, I shall desire my reader to compare what I have here written with what I have said in my twenty-first speculation.[1]   L.

SIR ROGER'S ANCESTORS.

[*STEELE, in SPECTATOR, No. 109. Thursday, July 5, 1711.*]

"Abnormis sapiens." [2]
HORACE, Lib. II. Sat. ii.

I WAS this morning walking in the gallery, when Sir Roger entered at the end opposite to me, and advancing towards me, said, he was glad to meet me among his relations the De Coverleys, and hoped I liked the conversation of so much good company, who were as silent as myself. I knew he alluded to the pictures, and as he is a gentleman who does not a little value himself upon his ancient descent, I expected he would give me some account of them. We were now arrived at the upper end

---

[1] This refers to the twenty-first number of the Spectator, in which Addison writes of the three professions of divinity, law, and physic, and says that "they are each of them overburdened with practitioners, and filled with multitudes of ingenious gentlemen that starve one another."

[2] "Of plain good sense, untutored in the schools."

of the gallery, when the knight faced towards one of the pictures, and as we stood before it, he entered into the matter, after his blunt way of saying things, as they occur to his imagination, without regular introduction, or care to preserve the appearance of chain of thought.

"It is," said he, "worth while to consider the force of dress; and how the persons of one age differ from those of another, merely by that only. One may observe also, that the general fashion of one age has been followed by one particular set of people in another, and by them preserved from one generation to another. Thus the vast jetting coat and small bonnet, which was the habit in Harry the Seventh's[1] time, is kept on in the yeomen of the guard; not without a good and politic view, because they look a foot taller, and a foot and a half broader: besides that the cap leaves the face expanded, and consequently more terrible, and fitter to stand at the entrance of palaces.

"This predecessor of ours, you see, is dressed after this manner, and his cheeks would be no larger than mine, were he in a hat as I am. He was the last man that won a prize in the Tilt-yard[2] (which is now a common street before Whitehall). You see the broken lance that lies there by his right foot; he shivered that lance of his adversary all to pieces; and bearing himself, look you, sir, in this manner, at the same time he came within the target of the gentleman who rode against him, and taking him with incredible force before him on the pommel of his saddle, he in that manner rid the tournament over, with an air that showed he did it rather to perform the rule of the lists, than expose his

[1] During the reign of Henry VII. (born, 1456; died, 1509), the first English king of the Tudor dynasty, the discovery of America and the invention of printing took place.

[2] This was an open space at Whitehall, the king's palace from Henry VIII. to William III., over against the banqueting-house, and included part of the present Parade in St. James's Park, London. Henry VIII. held a famous tourney there on May Day, 1540. During the reign of James I. there was tilting there on March 24, Prince Charles distinguishing himself.

enemy; however, it appeared he knew how to make use of a victory, and with a gentle trot he marched up to a gallery where their mistress sat (for they were rivals) and let him down with laudable courtesy and pardonable insolence. I don't know but it might be exactly where the coffee-house is now.

"You are to know this my ancestor was not only of a military genius, but fit also for the arts of peace, for he played on the bass viol as well as any gentlemen at court; you see where his viol hangs by his basket-hilt sword. The action at the Tilt-yard you may be sure won the fair lady, who was a maid of honor, and the greatest beauty of her time; here she stands, the next picture. You see, sir, my great-great-great-grandmother has on the new-fashioned petticoat, except that the modern is gathered at the waist; my grandmother appears as if she stood in a large drum, whereas the ladies now walk as if they were in a go-cart. For all this lady was bred at court, she became an excellent country wife, she brought ten children, and when I show you the library, you shall see in her own hand (allowing for the difference of the language) the best receipt now in England both for a hasty-pudding and a white-pot.[1]

"If you please to fall back a little, because 'tis necessary to look at the three next pictures at one view; these are three sisters. She on the right hand, who is so very beautiful, died a maid; the next to her, still handsomer, had the same fate, against her will; this homely thing in the middle had both their portions added to her own, and was stolen by a neighboring gentleman, a man of stratagem and resolution, for he poisoned three mastiffs to come at her, and knocked down two deer-stealers in carrying her off. Misfortunes happen in all families: the theft of this romp and so much money, was no great matter to our estate. But the next heir that possessed it was this soft gentleman, whom you see there: observe the small buttons, the little boots, the laces, the slashes about his clothes, and above all the posture he is drawn in, (which to be sure was his own choosing;) you see

---

[1] A kind of custard.

he sits with one hand on a desk writing, and looking as it were another way, like an easy writer, or a sonneteer: he was one of those that had too much wit to know how to live in the world; he was a man of no justice, but great good manners; he ruined everybody that had anything to do with him, but never said a rude thing in his life; the most indolent person in the world, he would sign a deed that passed away half his estate with his gloves on, but would not put on his hat before a lady if it were to save his country. He is said to be the first that made love by squeezing the hand. He left the estate with ten thousand pounds debt upon it, but however by all hands I have been informed that he was every way the finest gentleman in the world. That debt lay heavy on our house for one generation, but it was retrieved by a gift from that honest man you see there, a citizen of our name, but nothing at all akin to us. I know Sir Andrew Freeport has said behind my back, that this man was descended from one of the ten children of the maid of honor I showed you above; but it was never made out. We winked at the thing indeed, because money was wanting at that time."

Here I saw my friend a little embarrassed, and turned my face to the next portraiture.

Sir Roger went on with his account of the gallery in the following manner. "This man (pointing to him I looked at) I take to be the honor of our house. Sir Humphrey de Coverley; he was in his dealings as punctual as a tradesman, and as generous as a gentleman. He would have thought himself as much undone by breaking his word, as if it were to be followed by bankruptcy. He served his country as knight of this shire[1] to his dying day. He found it no easy matter to maintain an integrity in his words and actions, even in things that regarded the offices which were incumbent upon him, in the care of his own affairs and relations of life, and therefore dreaded (though he had great talents) to go into employments of state, where he must be ex-

---

[1] A knight of the shire was a knight chosen by the freeholders of a county to represent them in Parliament.

posed to the snares of ambition. Innocence of life and great ability were the distinguishing parts of his character; the latter, he had often observed, had led to the destruction of the former, and used frequently to lament that great and good had not the same signification. He was an excellent husbandman, but had resolved not to exceed such a degree of wealth; all above it he bestowed in secret bounties many years after the sum he aimed at for his own use was attained. Yet he did not slacken his industry, but to a decent old age spent the life and fortune which was superfluous to himself, in the service of his friends and neighbors."

Here we were called to dinner, and Sir Roger ended the discourse of this gentleman, by telling me, as we followed the servant, that this his ancestor was a brave man, and narrowly escaped being killed in the civil wars; "for," said he, "he was sent out of the field upon a private message, the day before the battle of Worcester." The whim of narrowly escaping by having been within a day of danger, with other matters above mentioned, mixed with good sense, left me at a loss whether I was more delighted with my friend's wisdom or simplicity. R.

NIGHT FEARS AT COVERLEY.

[*ADDISON, in SPECTATOR, No. 110. Friday, July 6, 1711.*]

"Horror ubique animos, simul ipsa silentia terrent." [1]
VIRGIL, Æneid, Lib. II. 755.

AT a little distance from Sir Roger's house, among the ruins of an old abbey, there is a long walk of aged elms; which are shot up so very high, that when one passes under them, the rooks and crows that rest upon the tops of them seem to be cawing in another region. I am very much delighted with this sort

[1] Dryden's translation: —
"All things are full of horror and affright,
And dreadful ev'n the silence of the night."

of noise, which I consider as a kind of natural prayer to that Being who supplies the wants of his whole creation, and who, in the beautiful language of the Psalms, feedeth the young ravens that call upon him. I like this retirement the better, because of an ill report it lies under of being haunted; for which reason (as I have been told in the family) no living creature ever walks in it besides the chaplain. My good friend the butler desired me with a very grave face not to venture myself in it after sunset, for that one of the footmen had been almost frighted out of his wits by a spirit that appeared to him in the shape of a black horse without a head; to which he added, that about a month ago one of the maids coming home late that way with a pail of milk upon her head, heard such a rustling among the bushes that she let it fall.

I was taking a walk in this place last night between the hours of nine and ten, and could not but fancy it one of the most proper scenes in the world for a ghost to appear in. The ruins of the abbey are scattered up and down on every side, and half covered with ivy and elder-bushes, the harbors of several solitary birds which seldom make their appearance till the dusk of the evening. The place was formerly a churchyard, and has still several marks in it of graves and burying-places. There is such an echo among the old ruins and vaults, that if you stamp but a little louder than ordinary, you hear the sound repeated. At the same time the walk of elms, with the croaking of the ravens which from time to time are heard from the tops of them, looks exceeding solemn and venerable. These objects naturally raise seriousness and attention; and when night heightens the awfulness of the place, and pours out her supernumerary horrors upon everything in it, I do not at all wonder that weak minds fill it with specters and apparitions.

Mr. Locke,[1] in his chapter of the Association of Ideas, has

---

[1] John Locke (1632–1704) was a celebrated English philosopher, and author of many works, the most famous being the Essay on the Human Understanding.

very curious remarks to show how by the prejudice of education one idea often introduces into the mind a whole set that bear no resemblance to one another in the nature of things. Among several examples of this kind, he produces the following instance. "The ideas of goblins and sprites have really no more to do with darkness than light: yet let but a foolish maid inculcate these often on the mind of a child, and raise them there together, possibly he shall never be able to separate them again so long as he lives; but darkness shall ever afterwards bring with it those frightful ideas, and they shall be so joined, that he can no more bear the one than the other."

As I was walking in this solitude, where the dusk of the evening conspired with so many other occasions of terror, I observed a cow grazing not far from me, which an imagination that is apt to startle might easily have construed into a black horse without a head: and I dare say the poor footman lost his wits upon some such trivial occasion.

My friend Sir Roger has often told me with a great deal of mirth, that at his first coming to his estate he found three parts of his house altogether useless; that the best room in it had the reputation of being haunted, and by that means was locked up; that noises had been heard in his long gallery, so that he could not get a servant to enter it after eight o'clock at night; that the door of one of his chambers was nailed up, because there went a story in the family that a butler had formerly hanged himself in it; and that his mother, who lived to a great age, had shut up half the rooms in the house, in which either her husband, a son, or daughter had died. The knight seeing his habitation reduced to so small a compass, and himself in a manner shut out of his own house, upon the death of his mother ordered all the apartments to be flung open, and exorcised by his chaplain, who lay in every room one after another, and by that means dissipated the fears which had so long reigned in the family.

I should not have been thus particular upon these ridiculous horrors, did I not find them so very much prevail in all parts of

the country. At the same time I think a person who is thus ter-
rified with the imagination of ghosts and specters much more
reasonable than one who, contrary to the reports of all historians
sacred and profane, ancient and modern, and to the traditions of
all nations, thinks the appearance of spirits fabulous and groundless: could not I give myself up to this general testimony of mankind, I should to the relations of particular persons who are now
living, and whom I cannot distrust in other matters of fact. I
might here add, that not only the historians, to whom we may
join the poets, but likewise the philosophers of antiquity have
favored this opinion. Lucretius himself, though by the course
of his philosophy he was obliged to maintain that the soul did
not exist separate from the body, makes no doubt of the reality
of apparitions, and that men have often appeared after their
death. This I think very remarkable; he was so pressed with
the matter of fact which he could not have the confidence to
deny, that he was forced to account for it by one of the most
absurd unphilosophical notions that was ever started. He tells
us, that the surfaces of all bodies are perpetually flying off from
their respective bodies, one after another; and that these surfaces
or thin cases that included each other whilst they were joined in
the body like the coats of an onion, are sometimes seen entire when
they are separated from it; by which means we often behold the
shapes and shadows of persons who are either dead or absent.

I shall dismiss this paper with a story out of Josephus,[1] not so
much for the sake of the story itself as for the moral reflections
with which the author concludes it, and which I shall here set
down in his own words. "Glaphyra the daughter of King
Archelaus, after the death of her two first husbands (being married to a third, who was brother to her first husband, and so pas-
sionately in love with her that he turned off his former wife to

---

[1] Flavius Josephus (born at Jerusalem, A.D. 37; date of death unknown)
was the most celebrated of Jewish historians. His chief works were, History of the Jewish War, in seven books; and Antiquities of the Jews, in
twenty books.

make room for this marriage) had a very odd kind of dream. She fancied that she saw her first husband coming towards her, and that she embraced him with great tenderness; when in the midst of the pleasure which she expressed at the sight of him, he reproached her after the following manner: ' Glaphyra,' says he, ' thou hast made good the old saying, that women are not to be trusted. Was not I the husband of thy virginity? Have I not children by thee? How couldst thou forget our loves so far as to enter into a second marriage, and after that into a third, nay to take for thy husband a man who has so shamelessly crept into the bed of his brother? However, for the sake of our past loves, I shall free thee from thy present reproach, and make thee mine forever.' Glaphyra told this dream to several women of her acquaintance, and died soon after." I thought this story might not be impertinent in this place, wherein I speak of those kings: besides that, the example deserves to be taken notice of as it contains a most certain proof of the immortality of the soul, and of Divine Providence. If any man thinks these facts incredible, let him enjoy his own opinion to himself, but let him not endeavor to disturb the belief of others, who by instances of this nature are excited to the study of virtue.   L.

A SUNDAY WITH SIR ROGER.

[*ADDISON, in SPECTATOR, No. 112. Monday, July 9, 1711.*]

" 'Αθανάτους μεν πρῶτα θεοὺς, νόμῳ ὡς διάκειται.
  Τιμᾶ." [1]
                                        PYTHAGORAS.

I AM always very well pleased with a country Sunday; and think, if keeping holy the seventh day were only a human institution, it would be the best method that could have been

[1] Free translation: —
    " First, in obedience to thy country's rites,
      Worship th' immortal gods."

thought of for the polishing and civilizing of mankind. It is certain the country people would soon degenerate into a kind of savages and barbarians, were there not such frequent returns of a stated time, in which the whole village meet together with their best faces, and in their cleanliest habits, to converse with one another upon indifferent subjects, hear their duties explained to them, and join together in adoration of the Supreme Being. Sunday clears away the rust of the whole week, not only as it refreshes in their minds the notions of religion, but as it puts both the sexes upon appearing in their most agreeable forms, and exerting all such qualities as are apt to give them a figure in the eye of the village. A country fellow distinguishes himself as much in the churchyard, as a citizen does upon the Change, the whole parish politics being generally discussed in that place either after sermon or before the bell rings.

My friend Sir Roger, being a good churchman, has beautified the inside of his church with several texts of his own choosing: he has likewise given a handsome pulpit-cloth, and railed in the communion-table at his own expense. He has often told me, that at his coming to his estate he found his parishioners very irregular; and that in order to make them kneel and join in the responses, he gave every one of them a hassock and a Common Prayer Book: and at the same time employed an itinerant singing-master, who goes about the country for that purpose, to instruct them rightly in the tunes of the Psalms; upon which they now very much value themselves, and indeed outdo most of the country churches that I have ever heard.

As Sir Roger is landlord to the whole congregation, he keeps them in very good order, and will suffer nobody to sleep in it besides himself; for if by chance he has been surprised into a short nap at sermon, upon recovering out of it he stands up and looks about him, and if he sees anybody else nodding, either wakes them himself, or sends his servant to them. Several other of the old knight's particularities break out upon these occasions: sometimes he will be lengthening out a verse in the singing Psalms, half a minute after the rest of the congregation have done with it; sometimes, when he is pleased with the matter of his devotion, he pronounces "Amen" three or four times to the same prayer; and sometimes stands up when everybody else is upon their knees, to count the congregation, or see if any of his tenants are missing.

I was yesterday very much surprised to hear my old friend, in the midst of the service, calling out to one John Matthews to mind what he was about, and not disturb the congregation. This John Matthews it seems is remarkable for being an idle fellow, and at that time was kicking his heels for his diversion. This authority of the knight, though exerted in that odd manner which accompanies him in all circumstances of life, has a very good effect upon the parish, who are not polite enough to see anything ridiculous in his behavior; besides that the general good sense and worthiness of his character makes his friends observe these little singularities as foils that rather set off than blemish his good qualities.

As soon as the sermon is finished, nobody presumes to stir till Sir Roger is gone out of the church. The knight walks down from his seat in the chancel between a double row of his tenants, that stand bowing to him on each side; and every now and then inquires how such a one's wife, or mother, or son, or father do, whom he does not see at church; which is understood as a secret reprimand to the person that is absent.

The chaplain has often told me, that upon a catechising day, when Sir Roger has been pleased with a boy that answers well, he has ordered a Bible to be given him next day for his encouragement; and sometimes accompanies it with a flitch of bacon to his mother. Sir Roger has likewise added five pounds a year to the clerk's place; and that he may encourage the young fellows to make themselves perfect in the church service, has promised upon the death of the present incumbent, who is very old, to bestow it according to merit.

The fair understanding between Sir Roger and his chaplain,

and their mutual concurrence in doing good, is the more remarkable, because the very next village is famous for the differences and contentions that rise between the parson and the squire, who live in a perpetual state of war. The parson is always preaching at the squire, and the squire to be revenged on the parson never comes to church. The squire has made all his tenants atheists and tithe-stealers; while the parson instructs them every Sunday in the dignity of his order, and insinuates to them in almost every sermon, that he is a better man than his patron. In short, matters are come to such an extremity, that the squire has not said his prayers either in public or private this half year; and that the parson threatens him, if he does not mend his manners, to pray for him in the face of the whole congregation.

Feuds of this nature, though too frequent in the country, are very fatal to the ordinary people; who are so used to be dazzled with riches, that they pay as much deference to the understanding of a man of an estate, as of a man of learning; and are very hardly brought to regard any truth, how important soever it may be, that is preached to them, when they know there are several men of five hundred a year who do not believe it.   L.

SIR ROGER IN LOVE.

[*STEELE, in SPECTATOR, No. 113. Tuesday, July 10, 1711.*]

"Hærent infixi pectore vultus." [1]
VIRGIL, Æneid, Lib. IV. 4.

IN my first description of the company in which I pass most of my time, it may be remembered that I mentioned a great affliction which my friend Sir Roger had met with in his youth; which was no less than a disappointment in love. It happened

---

[1] " Her looks were deep imprinted in his heart."

this evening, that we fell into a very pleasing walk at a distance from his house: as soon as we came into it, "It is," quoth the good old man, looking round him with a smile, "very hard, that any part of my land should be settled upon one who has used me so ill as the perverse widow did; and yet I am sure I could not see a sprig of any bough of this whole walk of trees, but I should reflect upon her and her severity. She has certainly the finest hand of any woman in the world. You are to know this was the place wherein I used to muse upon her; and by that custom I can never come into it, but the same tender sentiments revive in my mind, as if I had actually walked with that beautiful creature under these shades. I have been fool enough to carve her name on the bark of several of these trees; so unhappy is the condition of men in love, to attempt the removing of their passion by the methods which serve only to imprint it deeper. She has certainly the finest hand of any woman in the world."

Here followed a profound silence; and I was not displeased to observe my friend falling so naturally into a discourse, which I had ever before taken notice he industriously avoided. After a very long pause he entered upon an account of this great circumstance in his life, with an air which I thought raised my idea of him above what I had ever had before; and gave me the picture of that cheerful mind of his, before it received that stroke which has ever since affected his words and actions. But he went on as follows.

"I came to my estate in my twenty-second year, and resolved to follow the steps of the most worthy of my ancestors who have inhabited this spot of earth before me, in all the methods of hospitality and good neighborhood, for the sake of my fame; and in country sports and recreations, for the sake of my health. In my twenty-third year I was obliged to serve as sheriff of the county; and in my servants, officers and whole equipage, indulged the pleasure of a young man (who did not think ill of his own person) in taking that public occasion of showing my figure and behavior to advantage. You may easily imagine to yourself what appearance I made, who am pretty tall, rid well, and was very well dressed, at the head of a whole county, with music before me, a feather in my hat, and my horse well bitted. I can assure you I was not a little pleased with the kind looks and glances I had from all the balconies and windows as I rode to the hall where the assizes[1] were held. But when I came there, a beautiful creature in a widow's habit sat in court to hear the event of a cause concerning her dower. This commanding creature (who was born for destruction of all who behold her) put on such a resignation in her countenance, and bore the whispers of all around the court with such a pretty uneasiness, I warrant you, and then recovered herself from one eye to another, till she was perfectly confused by meeting something so wistful in all she encountered, that at last, with a murrain to her, she cast her bewitching eye upon me. I no sooner met it, but I bowed like a great surprised booby; and knowing her cause to be the first which came on, I cried, like a captivated calf as I was, ' Make way for the defendant's witnesses.' This sudden partiality made all the county immediately see the sheriff also was become a slave to the fine widow. During the time her cause was upon trial, she behaved herself, I warrant you, with such a deep attention to her business, took opportunities to have little billets handed to her counsel, then would be in such a pretty confusion, occasioned, you must know, by acting before so much company, that not only I but the whole court was prejudiced in her favor; and all that the next heir to her husband had to urge, was thought so groundless and frivolous, that when it came to her counsel to reply, there was not half so much said as every one besides in the court thought he could have urged to her advantage. You must understand, sir, this perverse woman is one of those unaccountable creatures, that secretly rejoice in the admiration of men, but indulge themselves in no further consequences. Hence it is that she has ever had a train of admirers, and she

---

[1] The periodical sessions of the judges of the superior courts in every county in England, for the trial of cases, and the administration of justice.

removes from her slaves in town to those in the country, according to the seasons of the year. She is a reading lady, and far gone in the pleasures of friendship; she is always accompanied by a confidante, who is witness to her daily protestations against our sex, and consequently a bar to her first steps towards love, upon the strength of her own maxims and declarations.

"However, I must needs say this accomplished mistress of mine has distinguished me above the rest, and has been known to declare Sir Roger de Coverley was the tamest and most human of all the brutes in the country. I was told she said so, by one who thought he rallied me; but upon the strength of this slender encouragement, of being thought least detestable, I made new liveries, new-paired my coach horses, sent them all to town to be bitted, and taught to throw their legs well, and move all together, before I pretended to cross the country and wait upon her. As soon as I thought my retinue suitable to the character of my fortune and youth, I set out from hence to make my addresses. The particular skill of this lady has ever been to inflame your wishes, and yet command respect. To make her mistress of this art, she has a greater share of knowledge, wit, and good sense, than is usual even among men of merit. Then she is beautiful beyond the race of women. If you won't let her go on with a certain artifice with her eyes, and the skill of beauty, she will arm herself with her real charms, and strike you with admiration instead of desire. It is certain that if you were to behold the whole woman, there is that dignity in her aspect, that composure in her motion, that complacency in her manner, that if her form makes you hope, her merit makes you fear. But then again, she is such a desperate scholar, that no country gentleman can approach her without being a jest. As I was going to tell you, when I came to her house I was admitted to her presence with great civility; at the same time she placed herself to be first seen by me in such an attitude, as I think you call the posture of a picture, that she discovered new charms, and I at last came towards her with such an awe as made me speechless. This she no sooner observed but she made her advantage of it, and began a discourse to me concerning love and honor, as they both are followed by pretenders, and the real votaries to them. When she had discussed these points in a discourse, which I verily believe was as learned as the best philosopher in Europe could possibly make, she asked me whether she was so happy as to fall in with my sentiments on these important particulars. Her confidante sat by her, and upon my being in the last confusion and silence, this malicious aid of hers, turning to her, says, ' I am very glad to observe Sir Roger pauses upon this subject, and seems resolved to deliver all his sentiments upon the matter when he pleases to speak.' They both kept their countenances, and after I had sat half an hour meditating how to behave before such profound casuists, I rose up and took my leave. Chance has since that time thrown me very often in her way, and she as often has directed a discourse to me which I do not understand. This barbarity has kept me ever at a distance from the most beautiful object my eyes ever beheld. It is thus also she deals with all mankind, and you must make love to her, as you would conquer the Sphinx,[1] by posing her. But were she like other women, and that there were any talking to her, how constant must the pleasure of that man be, who could converse with a creature — But, after all, you may be sure her heart is fixed on some one or other. They say she sings excellently : her voice in her ordinary speech has something in it inexpressibly sweet. You must know I dined with her at a public table the day after I first saw her, and she helped me to some tansy[2] in the eye of all the gentle-

---

[1] In Egyptian art, an image of granite or porphyry, having a human head, or the head of a ram or of a hawk, upon the wingless body of a lion ; in Grecian art, of similar design. The most famous Grecian Sphinx, that of Thebes in Bœotia, is said to have proposed a riddle to the Thebans, and killed those who were unable to guess it. The enigma was solved by Œdipus, whereupon the Sphinx slew herself.

[2] A dish common in the seventeenth century, made of eggs, sugar, rosewater, cream, and the juice of herbs, baked with butter in a shallow dish.

men in the country: she has certainly the finest hand of any woman in the world. I can assure you, sir, were you to behold her, you would be in the same condition; for as her speech is music, her form is angelic. But I find I grow irregular while I am talking of her: but indeed it would be stupidity to be unconcerned at such perfection. Oh the excellent creature, she is as inimitable to all women, as she is inaccessible to all men."

I found my friend begin to rave, and insensibly led him towards the house, that we might be joined by some other company; and am convinced that the widow is the secret cause of all that inconsistency which appears in some parts of my friend's discourse; though he has so much command of himself as not directly to mention her, yet according to that of Martial,[1] which one knows not how to render in English, *Dum tacet hanc loquitur.* I shall end this paper with that whole epigram, which represents with much humor my honest friend's condition.

> " Quicquid agit Rufus nihil est nisi Nævia Rufo,
>   Si gaudet, si flet, si tacet, hanc loquitur :
> Cœnat, propinat, poscit, negat, annuit, una est
>   Nævia ; si non sit Nævia mutus erit.
> Scriberet hesterna patri cum luce salutem,
>   Nævia lux, inquit, Nævia lumen, ave."[2]
>
>   Lib. I. Ep. 69, i.

                                                    R.

[1] A famous Latin epigrammatic poet, who was born in Spain about A. D. 40, but spent most of his life in Rome. He was a friend of Juvenal, Quintilian, and the Younger Pliny. He wrote epigrams chiefly, of which fourteen books are extant.

[2] Free translation : —

> " Let Rufus weep, rejoice, stand, sit, or walk,
>   Still he can nothing but of Nævia talk;
>   Let him eat, drink, ask questions, or dispute,
>   Still he must speak of Nævia, or be mute.
>   He writ to his father, ending with this line,
>   I am, my lovely Nævia, ever thine."

SIR ROGER'S ECONOMY.

[*STEELE, in SPECTATOR, No. 114. Wednesday, July 11 1711.*]

"*Paupertatis pudor et fuga.*" [1]
HORACE, Lib. I. Ep. xviii. 24.

ECONOMY in our affairs has the same effect upon our fortunes which good breeding has upon our conversations. There is a pretending behavior in both cases, which, instead of making men esteemed, renders them both miserable and contemptible. We had yesterday at Sir Roger's a set of country gentlemen who dined with him; and after dinner the glass was taken by those who pleased, pretty plentifully. Among others I observed a person of a tolerable good aspect, who seemed to be more greedy of liquor than any of the company, and yet, methought, he did not taste it with delight. As he grew warm, he was suspicious of everything that was said; and as he advanced towards being fuddled, his humor grew worse. At the same time his bitterness seemed to be rather an inward dissatisfaction in his own mind, than any dislike he had taken at the company. Upon hearing his name, I knew him to be a gentleman of a considerable fortune in this county, but greatly in debt. What gives the unhappy man this peevishness of spirit is, that his estate is dipped,[2] and is eating out with usury; and yet he has not the heart to sell any part of it. His proud stomach, at the cost of restless nights, constant inquietudes, danger of affronts, and a thousand nameless inconveniences, preserves this canker in his fortune, rather than it shall be said he is a man of fewer hundreds a year than he has been commonly reputed. Thus he endures

[1] Pooly's translation: —
" The dread of nothing more
Than to be thought necessitous and poor."
[2] Mortgaged.

the torment of poverty, to avoid the name of being less rich. If you go to his house you see great plenty; but served in a manner that shows it is all unnatural, and that the master's mind is not at home. There is a certain waste and carelessness in the air of everything, and the whole appears but a covered indigence, a magnificent poverty. That neatness and cheerfulness, which attends the table of him who lives within compass, is wanting, and exchanged for a libertine way of service in all about him.

This gentleman's conduct, though a very common way of management, is as ridiculous as that officer's would be, who had but few men under his command, and should take the charge of an extent of country rather than of a small pass. To pay for, personate, and keep in a man's hands, a greater estate than he really has, is of all others the most unpardonable vanity, and must in the end reduce the man who is guilty of it to dishonor. Yet if we look round us in any county of Great Britain, we shall see many in this fatal error; if that may be called by so soft a name, which proceeds from a false shame of appearing what they really are, when the contrary behavior would in a short time advance them to the condition which they pretend to.

Laertes has fifteen hundred pounds a year; which is mortgaged for six thousand pounds; but it is impossible to convince him that if he sold as much as would pay off that debt, he would save four shillings in the pound, which he gives for the vanity of being the reputed master of it. Yet if Laertes did this, he would, perhaps, be easier in his own fortune; but then Irus, a fellow of yesterday, who has but twelve hundred a year, would be his equal. Rather than this shall be, Laertes goes on to bring wellborn beggars into the world, and every twelvemonth charges his estate with at least one year's rent more by the birth of a child.

Laertes and Irus are neighbors, whose way of living are an abomination to each other. Irus is moved by the fear of poverty, and Laertes by the shame of it. Though the motive of action is of so near affinity in both, and may be resolved into this, "that to each of them poverty is the greatest of all evils," yet are their manners very widely different. Shame of poverty makes Laertes launch into unnecessary equipage, vain expense, and lavish entertainments; fear of poverty makes Irus allow himself only plain necessaries, appear without a servant, sell his own corn, attend his laborers, and be himself a laborer. Shame of poverty makes Laertes go every day a step nearer to it; and fear of poverty stirs up Irus to make every day some further progress from it.

These different motives produce the excesses which men are guilty of in the negligence of and provision for themselves. Usury, stockjobbing, extortion and oppression, have their seed in the dread of want; and vanity, riot and prodigality, from the shame of it: but both these excesses are infinitely below the pursuit of a reasonable creature. After we have taken care to command so much as is necessary for maintaining ourselves in the order of men suitable to our character, the care of superfluities is a vice no less extravagant, than the neglect of necessaries would have been before.

Certain it is that they are both out of Nature when she is followed with reason and good sense. It is from this reflection that I always read Mr. Cowley[1] with the greatest pleasure: his magnanimity is as much above that of other considerable men as his understanding; and it is a true distinguishing spirit in the elegant author who published his works, to dwell so much upon the temper of his mind and the moderation of his desires: by this means he has rendered his friend as amiable as famous. That state of life which bears the face of poverty with Mr. Cowley's "great vulgar,"[2] is admirably described; and it is no small satisfaction to those of the same turn of desire, that he produces the authority of the wisest men of the best age of the

---

[1] Abraham Cowley (1618–67) was a celebrated English poet. His prose essays are considered models of fine English.

[2] This expression occurs in Cowley's Paraphrase of Horace, Ode iii. 1 : —

> "Hence, ye profane, I hate ye all,
> Both the great vulgar and the small."

world, to strengthen his opinion of the ordinary pursuits of mankind.

It would methinks be no ill maxim of life, if according to that ancestor of Sir Roger, whom I lately mentioned, every man would point to himself what sum he would resolve not to exceed. He might by this means cheat himself into a tranquillity on this side of that expectation, or convert what he should get above it to nobler uses than his own pleasures or necessities. This temper of mind would exempt a man from an ignorant envy of restless men above him, and a more inexcusable contempt of happy men below him. This would be sailing by some compass, living with some design; but to be eternally bewildered in prospects of future gain, and putting on unnecessary armor against improbable blows of fortune, is a mechanic being which has not good sense for its direction, but is carried on by a sort of acquired instinct towards things below our consideration and unworthy our esteem. It is possible that the tranquillity I now enjoy at Sir Roger's may have created in me this way of thinking, which is so abstracted from the common relish of the world: but as I am now in a pleasing arbor surrounded with a beautiful landscape, I find no inclination so strong as to continue in these mansions, so remote from the ostentatious scenes of life; and am at this present writing philosopher enough to conclude with Mr. Cowley;

> " If e'er ambition did my fancy cheat,
>   With any wish so mean as to be great;
>   Continue, Heav'n, still from me to remove
>   The humble blessings of that life I love."

T.

BODILY EXERCISE.

[*ADDISON, in* SPECTATOR, *No. 115. Thursday, July 12, 1711.*]

" Ut sit mens sana in corpore sano." [1]
JUVENAL, Sat. x. 356.

BODILY labor is of two kinds, either that which a man submits to for his livelihood, or that which he undergoes for his pleasure. The latter of them generally changes the name of labor for that of exercise, but differs only from ordinary labor as it rises from another motive.

A country life abounds in both these kinds of labor, and for that reason gives a man a greater stock of health, and consequently a more perfect enjoyment of himself, than any other way of life. I consider the body as a system of tubes and glands, or to use a more rustic phrase, a bundle of pipes and strainers, fitted to one another after so wonderful a manner as to make a proper engine for the soul to work with. This description does not only comprehend the bowels, bones, tendons, veins, nerves and arteries, but every muscle and every ligature, which is a composition of fibers, that are so many imperceptible tubes or pipes interwoven on all sides with invisible glands or strainers.

This general idea of a human body, without considering it in its niceties of anatomy, lets us see how absolutely necessary labor is for the right preservation of it. There must be frequent motions and agitations, to mix, digest, and separate the juices contained in it, as well as to clear and cleanse that infinitude of pipes and strainers of which it is composed, and to give their solid parts a more firm and lasting tone. Labor or exercise ferments the humors, casts them into their proper channels, throws off redundancies, and helps Nature in those secret distributions, without which the body cannot subsist in its vigor, nor the soul act with cheerfulness.

---

[1] " Pray for a sound mind in a sound body."

I might here mention the effects which this has upon all the faculties of the mind, by keeping the understanding clear, the imagination untroubled, and refining those spirits that are necessary for the proper exertion of our intellectual faculties, during the present laws of union between soul and body. It is to a neglect in this particular that we must ascribe the spleen, which is so frequent in men of studious and sedentary tempers, as well as the vapors to which those of the other sex are so often subject.

Had not exercise been absolutely necessary for our well-being, Nature would not have made the body so proper for it, by giving such an activity to the limbs, and such a pliancy to every part as necessarily produce those compressions, extensions, contortions, dilatations, and all other kinds of motions that are necessary for the preservation of such a system of tubes and glands as has been before mentioned. And that we might not want inducements to engage us in such an exercise of the body as is proper for its welfare, it is so ordered that nothing valuable can be procured without it. Not to mention riches and honor, even food and raiment are not to be come at without the toil of the hands and sweat of the brows. Providence furnishes materials, but expects that we should work them up ourselves. The earth must be labored before it gives its increase, and when it is forced into its several products, how many hands must they pass through before they are fit for use? Manufactures, trade, and agriculture, naturally employ more than nineteen parts of the species in twenty; and as for those who are not obliged to labor, by the condition in which they are born, they are more miserable than the rest of mankind, unless they indulge themselves in that voluntary labor which goes by the name of exercise.

My friend Sir Roger has been an indefatigable man in business of this kind, and has hung several parts of his house with the trophies of his former labors. The walls of his great hall are covered with the horns of several kinds of deer that he has killed in the chase, which he thinks the most valuable furniture of his house, as they afford him frequent topics of discourse, and show that he has not been idle. At the lower end of the hall, is a large otter's skin stuffed with hay, which his mother ordered to be hung up in that manner, and the knight looks upon with great satisfaction, because it seems he was but nine years old when his dog killed him. A little room adjoining to the hall is a kind of arsenal filled with guns of several sizes and inventions, with which the knight has made great havoc in the woods, and destroyed many thousands of pheasants, partridges and wood-cocks. His stable doors are patched with noses that belonged to foxes of the knight's own hunting down. Sir Roger showed me one of them that for distinction sake has a brass nail struck through it, which cost him about fifteen hours' riding, carried him through half a dozen counties, killed him a brace of geldings, and lost above half his dogs. This the knight looks upon as one of the greatest exploits of his life. The perverse widow, whom I have given some account of, was the death of several foxes; for Sir Roger has told me that in the course of his amours he patched the western door of his stable. Whenever the widow was cruel, the foxes were sure to pay for it. In proportion as his passion for the widow abated and old age came on, he left off fox-hunting; but a hare is not yet safe that sits within ten miles of his house.

There is no kind of exercise which I would so recommend to my readers of both sexes as this of riding, as there is none which so much conduces to health, and is every way accommodated to the body, according to the idea which I have given of it. Dr. Sydenham[1] is very lavish in its praises; and if the English reader will see the mechanical effects of it described at length, he may find them in a book published not many years since, under the title of "Medicina Gymnastica."[2] For my own part, when I am in

---

[1] Thomas Sydenham (1624–89) was a celebrated English physician. He wrote many valuable medical treatises.

[2] *Medicina Gymnastica* (Bodily Exercise as a Medicine). Published in 1704. Written by Francis Fuller, a Nonconformist clergyman, who died in 1701. By some the book is credited to Thomas Fuller, M.D.

town, for want of these opportunities, I exercise myself an hour every morning upon a dumb-bell that is placed in a corner of my room, and pleases me the more because it does everything I require of it in the most profound silence. My landlady and her daughters are so well acquainted with my hours of exercise, that they never come into my room to disturb me whilst I am ringing.

When I was some years younger than I am at present, I used to employ myself in a more laborious diversion, which I learned from a Latin treatise of exercises that is written with great erudition: it is there called the σκιομαχία, or the fighting with a man's own shadow, and consists in the brandishing of two short sticks grasped in each hand, and loaden with plugs of lead at either end. This opens the chest, exercises the limbs, and gives a man all the pleasure of boxing, without the blows. I could wish that several learned men would lay out that time which they employ in controversies and disputes about nothing, in this method of fighting with their own shadows. It might conduce very much to evaporate the spleen, which makes them uneasy to the public as well as to themselves.

To conclude, as I am a compound of soul and body, I consider myself as obliged to a double scheme of duties; and I think I have not fulfilled the business of the day when I do not thus employ the one in labor and exercise, as well as the other in study and contemplation.   L.

SIR ROGER AND THE CHASE.

[BUDGELL, in SPECTATOR, No. 116. Friday, July 13, 1711.]

"*Vocat ingenti clamore Cithæron,
     Taygetique canes.*" [1]
                          VIRGIL, Georgics, iii.

THOSE who have searched into human nature observe that nothing so much shows the nobleness of the soul, as that its felicity consists in action. Every man has such an active principle in him, that he will find out something to employ himself upon in whatever place or state of life he is posted. I have heard of a gentleman who was under close confinement in the Bastile seven years; during which time he amused himself in scattering a few small pins about his chamber, gathering them up again, and placing them in different figures on the arm of a great chair. He often told his friends afterwards, that unless he had found out this piece of exercise, he verily believed he should have lost his senses.

After what has been said, I need not inform my readers, that Sir Roger, with whose character I hope they are at present pretty well acquainted, has in his youth gone through the whole course of those rural diversions which the country abounds in; and which seem to be extremely well suited to that laborious industry a man may observe here in a far greater degree than in towns and cities. I have before hinted at some of my friend's exploits: he has in his youthful days taken forty coveys of partridges in a season; and tired many a salmon with a line consisting but of a single hair. The constant thanks and good wishes of the neighborhood always attended him, on account of his remarkable enmity towards foxes; having destroyed more of those vermin in one year, than it was thought the whole country could have pro-

1 " The echoing hills and chiding hounds invite."

duced. Indeed the knight does not scruple to own among his most intimate friends that in order to establish his reputation this way, he has secretly sent for great numbers of them out of other counties, which he used to turn loose about the country by night, that he might the better signalize himself in their destruction the next day. His hunting horses were the finest and best managed in all these parts: his tenants are still full of the praises of a gray stone-horse that unhappily staked himself several years since, and was buried with great solemnity in the orchard.

Sir Roger, being at present too old for fox-hunting, to keep himself in action, has disposed of his beagles and got a pack of stop-hounds.[1] What these want in speed, he endeavors to make amends for by the deepness of their mouths and the variety of their notes, which are suited in such manner to each other, that the whole cry makes up a complete consort. He is so nice in this particular that a gentleman having made him a present of a very fine hound the other day, the knight returned it by the servant with a great many expressions of civility; but desired him to tell his master, that the dog he had sent was indeed a most excellent bass, but that at present he only wanted a counter-tenor. Could I believe my friend had ever read Shakespeare, I should certainly conclude he had taken the hint from Theseus in the "Midsummer Night's Dream."

> " My hounds are bred out of the Spartan kind;
> So flew'd, so sanded; and their heads are hung
> With ears that sweep away the morning dew;
> Crook-kneed, and dew-lapp'd like Thessalian bulls;
> Slow in pursuit, but match'd in mouth like bells,
> Each under each. A cry more tunable
> Was never halloo'd to, nor cheer'd with horn."
>
> ACT iv. sc. I.

Sir Roger is so keen at this sport, that he has been out almost every day since I came down; and upon the chaplain's offering

---

[1] A beagle is a small hound used for hunting hares; a stop-hound, a dog trained to hunt slowly, stopping at the huntsman's signal.

to lend me his easy pad, I was prevailed on yesterday morning
to make one of the company. I was extremely pleased, as we
rid[1] along, to observe the general benevolence of all the neighborhood towards my friend. The farmers' sons thought themselves happy if they could open a gate for the good old knight
as he passed by; which he generally requited with a nod or a
smile, and a kind inquiry after their fathers and uncles.

After we had rid about a mile from home, we came upon a
large heath, and the sportsmen began to beat. They had done
so for some time, when, as I was at a little distance from the rest
of the company, I saw a hare pop out from a small furze-brake
almost under my horse's feet. I marked the way she took, which
I endeavored to make the company sensible of by extending my
arm; but to no purpose, till Sir Roger, who knows that none of
my extraordinary motions are insignificant, rode up to me, and
asked me if puss was gone that way? Upon my answering
"Yes," he immediately called in the dogs, and put them upon the
scent. As they were going off, I heard one of the country fellows muttering to his companion, that it was a wonder they had
not lost all their sport, for want of the silent gentleman's crying
"Stole away."

This, with my aversion to leaping hedges, made me withdraw
to a rising ground, from whence I could have the picture of the
whole chase, without the fatigue of keeping in with the hounds.
The hare immediately threw them above a mile behind her; but
I was pleased to find, that instead of running straight forwards,
or in hunter's language, "flying the country," as I was afraid
she might have done, she wheeled about, and described a sort of
circle round the hill where I had taken my station, in such manner as gave me a very distinct view of the sport. I could see
her first pass by, and the dogs some time afterwards unraveling
the whole track she had made, and following her through all her
doubles. I was at the same time delighted in observing that
deference which the rest of the pack paid to each particular

---

[1] The old form of the past tense of the verb "to ride."

hound, according to the character he had acquired amongst them: if they were at fault, and an old hound of reputation opened but once, he was immediately followed by the whole cry; while a raw dog or one who was a noted liar, might have yelped his heart out, without being taken notice of.

The hare now, after having squatted two or three times, and been put up again as often, came still nearer to the place where she was at first started. The dogs pursued her, and these were followed by the jolly knight, who rode upon a white gelding, encompassed by his tenants and servants, and cheering his hounds with all the gayety of five and twenty. One of the sportsmen rode up to me, and told me, that he was sure the chase was almost at an end, because the old dogs, which had hitherto lain behind, now headed the pack. The fellow was in the right. Our hare took a large field just under us, followed by the full cry in view. I must confess the brightness of the weather, the cheerfulness of everything around me, the chiding of the hounds, which was returned upon us in a double echo, from two neighboring hills, with the hallooing of the sportsmen, and the sounding of the horn, lifted my spirits into a most lively pleasure, which I freely indulged because I was sure it was innocent. If I was under any concern, it was on the account of the poor hare, that was now quite spent, and almost within the reach of her enemies; when the huntsman getting forward threw down his pole before the dogs. They were now within eight yards of that game which they had been pursuing for almost as many hours; yet on the signal before mentioned they all made a sudden stand, and though they continued opening as much as before, durst not once attempt to pass beyond the pole. At the same time Sir Roger rode forward, and alighting, took up the hare in his arms; which he soon delivered up to one of his servants with an order, if she could be kept alive, to let her go in his great orchard; where it seems he has several of these prisoners of war, who live together in a very comfortable captivity. I was highly pleased to see the discipline of the pack, and the good nature of the knight, who could not find in his heart to murder a creature that had given him so much diversion.

As we were returning home, I remembered that Monsieur Paschal[1] in his most excellent discourse on the misery of man, tells us, that all our endeavors after greatness proceed from nothing but a desire of being surrounded by a multitude of persons and affairs that may hinder us from looking into ourselves, which is a view we cannot bear. He afterwards goes on to show that our love of sports comes from the same reason, and is particularly severe upon hunting. "What," says he, "unless it be to drown thought, can make men throw away so much time and pains upon a silly animal, which they might buy cheaper in the market?" The foregoing reflection is certainly just, when a man suffers his whole mind to be drawn into his sports, and altogether loses himself in the woods; but does not affect those who propose a far more laudable end from this exercise, I mean, the preservation of health, and keeping all the organs of the soul in a condition to execute her orders. Had that incomparable person, whom I last quoted, been a little more indulgent to himself in this point, the world might probably have enjoyed him much longer; whereas through too great an application to his studies in his youth, he contracted that ill habit of body, which, after a tedious sickness, carried him off in the fortieth year of his age; and the whole history we have of his life till that time, is but one continued account of the behavior of a noble soul struggling under innumerable pains and distempers.

For my own part I intend to hunt twice a week during my stay with Sir Roger; and shall prescribe the moderate use of this exercise to all my country friends, as the best kind of physic for mending a bad constitution, and preserving a good one.

I cannot do this better, than in the following lines out of Mr. Dryden.[2]

---

[1] Blaise Paschal (1623–62) was a noted French philosopher and mathematician. His best-known works are Thoughts, and Provincial Letters.

[2] John Dryden (1631–1700) was an eminent English poet and dramatist. Besides writing many plays, he translated Virgil and Juvenal.

"The first physicians by debauch were made;
Excess began, and Sloth sustains the trade.
By chase our long-liv'd fathers earn'd their food;
Toil strung the nerves, and purified the blood;
But we their sons, a pamper'd race of men,
Are dwindled down to threescore years and ten.
Better to hunt in fields for health unbought,
Than fee the doctor for a nauseous draught.
The wise for cure on exercise depend:
God never made his work for man to mend."

X.

MOLL WHITE,[1] THE WITCH.

[*Addison, in Spectator, No. 117. Saturday, July 14, 1711.*]

"*Ipsi sibi somnia fingunt.*"[2]
Virgil, Eclogues, viii. 108.

THERE are some opinions in which a man should stand neuter, without engaging his assent to one side or the other. Such a hovering faith as this, which refuses to settle upon any determination, is absolutely necessary to a mind that is careful to avoid errors and prepossessions. When the arguments press equally on both sides in matters that are indifferent to us, the safest method is to give up ourselves to neither.

It is with this temper of mind that I consider the subject of witchcraft. When I hear the relations that are made from all parts of the world, not only from Norway and Lapland, from the East and West Indies, but from every particular nation in Europe, I cannot forbear thinking that there is such an intercourse and commerce with evil spirits, as that which we express by the name of witchcraft. But when I consider that the igno-

[1] This character represents the belief in witchcraft current in England in the seventeenth century.
[2] "With voluntary dreams they cheat their minds."

rant and credulous parts of the world abound most in these relations, and that the persons among us, who are supposed to engage
in such an infernal commerce, are people of a weak understanding and a crazed imagination, and at the same time reflect
upon the many impostures and delusions of this nature that have
been detected in all ages, I endeavor to suspend my belief till
I hear more certain accounts than any which have yet come to
my knowledge. In short, when I consider the question, whether
there are such persons in the world as those we call witches, my
mind is divided between the two opposite opinions; or rather (to
speak my thoughts freely) I believe in general that there is, and
has been such a thing as witchcraft; but at the same time can
give no credit to any particular instance of it.

I am engaged in this speculation, by some occurrences that I
met with yesterday, which I shall give my reader an account of
at large. As I was walking with my friend Sir Roger by the
side of one of his woods, an old woman applied herself to me for
my charity. Her dress and figure put me in mind of the following description in Otway.[1]

> " In a close lane as I pursu'd my journey,
> I spy'd a wrinkled hag, with age grown double,
> Picking dry sticks, and mumbling to herself.
> Her eyes with scalding rheum were gall'd and red,
> Cold palsy shook her head; her hands seem'd wither'd;
> And on her crooked shoulders had she wrapp'd
> The tatter'd remnants of an old striped hanging,
> Which served to keep her carcass from the cold:
> So there was nothing of a piece about her.
> Her lower weeds were all o'er coarsely patch'd
> With diff'rent-color'd rags, black, red, white, yellow,
> And seem'd to speak variety of wretchedness."

As I was musing on this description, and comparing it with
the object before me, the knight told me, that this very old
woman had the reputation of a witch all over the country, that

---

[1] Thomas Otway (1651–85) was a well-known English dramatist.

her lips were observed to be always in motion, and that there was not a switch about her house which her neighbors did not believe had carried her several hundreds of miles. If she chanced to stumble, they always found sticks or straws that lay in the figure of a cross before her. If she made any mistake at church, and cried "Amen" in a wrong place, they never failed to conclude that she was saying her prayers backwards. There was not a maid in the parish that would take a pin of her, though she would offer a bag of money with it. She goes by the name of Moll White, and has made the country ring with several imaginary exploits which are palmed upon her. If the dairy-maid does not make her butter come so soon as she should have it, Moll White is at the bottom of the churn. If a horse sweats in the stable, Moll White has been upon his back. If a hare makes an unexpected escape from the hounds, the huntsman curses Moll White. Nay, (says Sir Roger) I have known the master of the pack, upon such an occasion, send one of his servants to see if Moll White had been out that morning.

This account raised my curiosity so far, that I begged my friend Sir Roger to go with me into her hovel, which stood in a solitary corner under the side of the wood. Upon our first entering Sir Roger winked to me, and pointed at something that stood behind the door, which, upon looking that way, I found to be an old broom-staff. At the same time he whispered me in the ear to take notice of a tabby cat that sat in the chimney-corner, which, as the old knight told me, lay under as bad a report as Moll White herself; for besides that Moll is said often to accompany her in the same shape, the cat is reported to have spoken twice or thrice in her life, and to have played several pranks above the capacity of an ordinary cat.

I was secretly concerned to see human nature in so much wretchedness and disgrace, but at the same time could not forbear smiling to hear Sir Roger, who is a little puzzled about the old woman, advising her as a justice of peace to avoid all communication with the Devil, and never to hurt any of her neighbors' cattle.   We concluded our visit with a bounty, which was very acceptable.

In our return home, Sir Roger told me, that old Moll had been often brought before him for making children spit pins, and giving maids the nightmare; and that the country people would be tossing her into a pond and trying experiments with her every day, if it was not for him and his chaplain.

I have since found upon inquiry, that Sir Roger was several times staggered with the reports that had been brought him concerning this old woman, and would frequently have bound her over to the county sessions, had not his chaplain with much ado persuaded him to the contrary.

I have been the more particular in this account, because I hear there is scarce a village in England that has not a Moll White in it.   When an old woman begins to dote, and grow chargeable to a parish, she is generally turned into a witch, and fills the whole country with extravagant fancies, imaginary distempers and terrifying dreams.   In the mean time, the poor wretch that is the innocent occasion of so many evils begins to be frighted at herself, and sometimes confesses secret commerce and familiarities that her imagination forms in a delirious old age.   This frequently cuts off charity from the greatest objects of compassion, and inspires people with a malevolence towards those poor decrepit parts of our species, in whom human nature is defaced by infirmity and dotage.   L.

LOVE–MAKING AT COVERLEY.

[*STEELE, in* SPECTATOR, *No. 118. Monday, July 16, 1711.*]

"Hæret lateri lethalis arundo." [1]
VIRGIL, Æneid, Lib. IV. 73.

THIS agreeable seat is surrounded with so many pleasing walks, which are struck out of a wood, in the midst of which the house stands, that one can hardly ever be weary of rambling from one labyrinth of delight to another. To one used to live in a city the charms of the country are so exquisite, that the mind is lost in a certain transport which raises us above ordinary life, and is yet not strong enough to be inconsistent with tranquillity. This state of mind was I in, ravished with the murmur of waters, the whisper of breezes, the singing of birds; and whether I looked up to the heavens, down on the earth, or turned to the prospects around me, still struck with new sense of pleasure; when I found by the voice of my friend, who walked by me, that we had insensibly strolled into the grove sacred to the widow. "This woman," says he, "is of all others the most unintelligible: she either designs to marry, or she does not. What is the most perplexing of all, is, that she doth not either say to her lovers she has any resolution against that condition of life in general, or that she banishes them; but conscious of her own merit, she permits their addresses, without fear of any ill consequence, or want of respect, from their rage or despair. She has that in her aspect, against which it is impossible to offend. A man whose thoughts are constantly bent upon so agreeable an object, must be excused if the ordinary occurrences in conversation are below his attention. I call her indeed perverse, but, alas! why do I call her so? Because her superior merit is such,

---

[1] Dryden's translation : —

"The fatal dart
Sticks in his side, and rankles in his heart,"

that I cannot approach her without awe, that my heart is checked by too much esteem: I am angry that her charms are not more accessible, that I am more inclined to worship than salute her: how often have I wished her unhappy that I might have an opportunity of serving her? and how often troubled in that very imagination, at giving her the pain of being obliged? Well, I have led a miserable life in secret upon her account; but fancy she would have condescended to have some regard for me, if it had not been for that watchful animal her confidante.

"Of all persons under the sun" (continued he, calling me by my name) "be sure to set a mark upon confidantes: they are of all people the most impertinent. What is most pleasant to observe in them, is, that they assume to themselves the merit of the persons whom they have in their custody. Orestilla is a great fortune, and in wonderful danger of surprises, therefore full of suspicions of the least indifferent thing, particularly careful of new acquaintance, and of growing too familiar with the old. Themista, her favorite woman, is every whit as careful of whom she speaks to, and what she says. Let the ward be a beauty, her confidante shall treat you with an air of distance; let her be a fortune, and she assumes the suspicious behavior of her friend and patroness. Thus it is that very many of our unmarried women of distinction, are to all intents and purposes married, except the consideration of different sexes. They are directly under the conduct of their whisperer; and think they are in a state of freedom, while they can prate with one of these attendants of all men in general, and still avoid the man they most like. You do not see one heiress in a hundred whose fate does not turn upon this circumstance of choosing a confidante. Thus it is that the lady is addressed to, presented and flattered, only by proxy, in her woman. In my case, how is it possible that "— Sir Roger was proceeding in his harangue, when we heard the voice of one speaking very importunately, and repeating these words, "What, not one smile?" We followed the sound till we came to a close thicket, on the other side of which we saw a young woman sitting

as it were in a personated sullenness just over a transparent
fountain. Opposite to her stood Mr. William, Sir Roger's master
of the game. The knight whispered me, " Hist, these are lovers."
The huntsman looking earnestly at the shadow of the young
maiden in the stream, " O thou dear picture, if thou couldst re-
main there in the absence of that fair creature whom you represent in the water, how willingly could I stand here satisfied forever, without troubling my dear Betty herself with any mention
of her unfortunate William, whom she is angry with: but alas!
when she pleases to be gone, thou wilt also vanish — Yet let
me talk to thee while thou dost stay. Tell my dearest Betty
thou dost not more depend upon her, than does her William?
Her absence will make away with me as well as thee. If she
offers to remove thee, I'll jump into these waves to lay hold on
thee; herself, her own dear person, I must never embrace again —
Still do you hear me without one smile — It is too much to
bear "— He had no sooner spoke these words, but he made
an offer of throwing himself into the water : at which his mistress
started up, and at the next instant he jumped across the fountain
and met her in an embrace. She half recovering from her fright,
said in the most charming voice imaginable, and with a tone of
complaint, " I thought how well you would drown yourself. No,
no, you won't drown yourself till you have taken your leave of
Susan Holliday." The huntsman, with a tenderness that spoke
the most passionate love, and with his cheek close to hers, whispered the softest vows of fidelity in her ear, and cried, " Don't,
my dear, believe a word Kate Willow says; she is spiteful and
makes stories, because she loves to hear me talk to herself for
your sake."—" Look you there," quoth Sir Roger, "do you see
there, all mischief comes from confidantes! But let us not inter-
rupt them ; the maid is honest, and the man dares not be otherwise, for he knows I loved her father: I will interpose in this
matter, and hasten the wedding. Kate Willow is a witty mis-
chievous wench in the neighborhood, who was a beauty ; and
makes me hope I shall see the perverse widow in her condition.

She was so flippant with her answers to all the honest fellows that came near her, and so very vain of her beauty, that she has valued herself upon her charms till they are ceased. She therefore now makes it her business to prevent other young women from being more discreet than she was herself: however, the saucy thing said the other day well enough, 'Sir Roger and I must make a match, for we are both despised by those we loved:' the hussy has a great deal of power wherever she comes, and has her share of cunning.

"However, when I reflect upon this woman, I do not know whether in the main I am the worse for having loved her: whenever she is recalled to my imagination my youth returns, and I feel a forgotten warmth in my veins. This affliction in my life has streaked all my conduct with a softness, of which I should otherwise have been incapable. It is, perhaps, to this dear image in my heart owing, that I am apt to relent, that I easily forgive, and that many desirable things are grown into my temper, which I should not have arrived at by better motives than the thought of being one day hers. I am pretty well satisfied such a passion as I have had is never well cured; and between you and me, I am often apt to imagine it has had some whimsical effect upon my brain: for I frequently find, that in my most serious discourse I let fall some comical familiarity of speech or odd phrase that makes the company laugh; however, I cannot but allow she is a most excellent woman. When she is in the country I warrant she does not run into dairies, but reads upon the nature of plants; but has a glass hive, and comes into the garden out of books to see them work, and observe the policies of their commonwealth. She understands everything. I'd give ten pounds to hear her argue with my friend Sir Andrew Freeport about trade. No, no, for all she looks so innocent, as it were, take my word for it she is no fool."   T.

COUNTRY MANNERS.

[*ADDISON, in SPECTATOR, No. 119. Tuesday, July 17, 1711.*]

" Urbem quam dicunt Romam, Meliboee, putavi
Stultus ego huic nostræ similem." [1]
VIRGIL, Eclogues, i. 20.

THE first and most obvious reflections which arise in a man
who changes the city for the country, are upon the different
manners of the people whom he meets with in those two different
scenes of life. By manners I do not mean morals, but behavior
and good breeding, as they show themselves in the town and in
the country.

And here, in the first place, I must observe a very great revolution that has happened in this article of good breeding. Several obliging deferences, condescensions and submissions, with
many outward forms and ceremonies that accompany them, were
first of all brought up among the politer part of mankind, who
lived in courts and cities, and distinguished themselves from the
rustic part of the species (who on all occasions acted bluntly and
naturally) by such a mutual complaisance and intercourse of
civilities. These forms of conversation by degrees multiplied and
grew troublesome; the modish world found too great a con-
straint in them, and have therefore thrown most of them aside.
Conversation, like the Romish religion, was so encumbered with
show and ceremony, that it stood in need of a reformation to
retrench its superfluities, and restore it to its natural good sense
and beauty. At present therefore an unconstrained carriage, and
a certain openness of behavior, are the height of good breeding.
The fashionable world is grown free and easy; our manners sit
more loose upon us: nothing is so modish as an agreeable negli-

[1] Warton's translation : —

" The city men call Rome, unskillful clown,
I thought resembled this our humble town."

gence. In a word, good breeding shows itself most, where to an ordinary eye it appears the least.

If after this we look on the people of mode in the country, we find in them the manners of the last age. They have no sooner fetched themselves up to the fashion of the polite world, but the town has dropped them, and are nearer to the first state of nature than to those refinements which formerly reigned in the court, and still prevail in the country. One may now know a man that never conversed in the world, by his excess of good breeding. A polite country squire shall make you as many bows in half an hour, as would serve a courtier for a week. There is infinitely more to do about place and precedency in a meeting of justices' wives, than in an assembly of duchesses.

This rural politeness is very troublesome to a man of my temper, who generally take the chair that is next me, and walk first or last, in the front or in the rear, as chance directs. I have known my friend Sir Roger's dinner almost cold before the company could adjust the ceremonial, and be prevailed upon to sit down; and have heartily pitied my old friend, when I have seen him forced to pick and cull his guests, as they sat at the several parts of his table, that he might drink their healths according to their respective ranks and qualities. Honest Will Wimble, who I should have thought had been altogether uninfected with ceremony, gives me abundance of trouble in this particular. Though he has been fishing all the morning, he will not help himself at dinner till I am served. When we are going out of the hall, he runs behind me; and last night, as we were walking in the fields, stopped short at a stile till I came up to it, and upon my making signs to him to get over, told me, with a serious smile, that sure I believed they had no manners in the country.

There has happened another revolution in the point of good breeding, which relates to the conversation among men of mode, and which I cannot but look upon as very extraordinary. It was certainly one of the first distinctions of a well-bred man, to express everything that had the most remote appearance of being obscene, in modest terms and distant phrases; whilst the clown, who had no such delicacy of conception and expression, clothed his ideas in those plain homely terms that are the most obvious and natural. This kind of good manners was perhaps carried to an excess, so as to make conversation too stiff, formal and precise; for which reason (as hypocrisy in one age is generally succeeded by atheism in another) conversation is in a great measure relapsed into the first extreme; so that at present several of our men of the town, and particularly those who have been polished in France, make use of the most coarse uncivilized words in our language, and utter themselves often in such a manner as a clown would blush to hear.

This infamous piece of good breeding, which reigns among the coxcombs of the town, has not yet made its way into the country; and as it is impossible for such an irrational way of conversation to last long among a people that make any profession of religion, or show of modesty, if the country gentlemen get into it they will certainly be left in the lurch. Their good breeding will come too late to them, and they will be thought a parcel of lewd clowns, while they fancy themselves talking together like men of wit and pleasure.

As the two points of good breeding, which I have hitherto insisted upon, regard behavior and conversation, there is a third which turns upon dress. In this too the country are very much behindhand. The rural beaus are not yet got out of the fashion that took place at the time of the Revolution, but ride about the country in red coats and laced hats, while the women in many parts are still trying to outvie one another in the height of their head-dresses.

But a friend of mine, who is now upon the western circuit,[1] having promised to give me an account of the several modes and fashions that prevail in the different parts of the nation through which he passes, I shall defer the enlarging upon this last topic till I have received a letter from him, which I expect every post.

L.

[1] One of the eight judicial divisions of England and Wales.

SIR ROGER'S POULTRY.

[*ADDISON, in SPECTATOR, No. 120. Wednesday, July 18, 1711.*]

> "*Equidem credo, quia sit divinitus illis
> Ingenium.*" [1]
> VIRGIL, Georgics, i. 451.

MY friend Sir Roger is very often merry with me upon my passing so much of my time among his poultry: he has caught me twice or thrice looking after a bird's-nest, and several times sitting an hour or two together near a hen and chickens. He tells me he believes I am personally acquainted with every fowl about his house; calls such a particular cock my favorite, and frequently complains that his ducks and geese have more of my company than himself.

I must confess I am infinitely delighted with those speculations of nature which are to be made in a country life; and as my reading has very much lain among books of natural history, I cannot forbear recollecting upon this occasion the several remarks which I have met with in authors, and comparing them with what falls under my own observation: the arguments for Providence drawn from the natural history of animals being in my opinion demonstrative.

The make of every kind of animal is different from that of every other kind; and yet there is not the least turn in the muscles or twist in the fibers of any one, which does not render them more proper for that particular animal's way of life than any other cast or texture of them would have been.

The most violent appetites in all creatures are lust and hunger: the first is a perpetual call upon them to propagate their kind; the latter to preserve themselves.

---

[1] Free translation:—

> " I deem their breasts inspir'd
> With a divine sagacity."

It is astonishing to consider the different degrees of care that descend from the parent to the young, so far as is absolutely necessary for the leaving a posterity. Some creatures cast their eggs as chance directs them, and think of them no further, as insects and several kinds of fish: others, of a nicer frame, find out proper beds to deposit them in, and there leave them; as the serpent, the crocodile, and ostrich: others hatch their eggs and tend the birth, till it is able to shift for itself.

What can we call the principle which directs every different kind of bird to observe a particular plan in the structure of its nest, and directs all of the same species to work after the same model? It cannot be imitation; for though you hatch a crow under a hen, and never let it see any of the works of its own kind, the nest it makes shall be the same, to the laying of a stick, with all the other nests of the same species. It cannot be reason; for were animals endued with it to as great a degree as man, their buildings would be as different as ours, according to the different conveniences that they would propose to themselves.

Is it not remarkable, that the same temper of weather, which raises this genial warmth in animals, should cover the trees with leaves and the fields with grass for their security and conceal-ment, and produce such infinite swarms of insects for the sup-port and sustenance of their respective broods?

Is it not wonderful, that the love of the parent should be so violent while it lasts; and that it should last no longer than is necessary for the preservation of the young?

But notwithstanding this natural love in brutes is much more violent and intense than in rational creatures, Providence has taken care that it should be no longer troublesome to the parent than it is useful to the young: for so soon as the wants of the latter cease, the mother withdraws her fondness, and leaves them to provide for themselves: and what is a very remarkable cir-cumstance in this part of instinct, we find that the love of the parent may be lengthened out beyond its usual time, if the pres-ervation of the species requires it; as we may see in birds that drive away their young as soon as they are able to get their live-lihood, but continue to feed them if they are tied to the nest, or confined within a cage, or by any other means appear to be out of a condition of supplying their own necessities.

This natural love is not observed in animals to ascend from the young to the parent, which is not at all necessary for the continuance of the species: nor indeed in reasonable creatures does it rise in any proportion, as it spreads itself downwards; for in all family affection, we find protection granted and favors bestowed, are greater motives to love and tenderness, than safety, benefits, or life received.

One would wonder to hear skeptical men disputing for the reason of animals, and telling us it is only our pride and preju-dices that will not allow them the use of that faculty.

Reason shows itself in all occurrences of life; whereas the brute makes no discovery of such a talent, but in what imme-diately regards his own preservation, or the continuance of his species. Animals in their generation are wiser than the sons of men; but their wisdom is confined to a few particulars, and lies in a very narrow compass. Take a brute out of his instinct, and you find him wholly deprived of understanding, To use an instance that comes often under observation.

With what caution does the hen provide herself a nest in places unfrequented, and free from noise and disturbance! When she has laid her eggs in such a manner that she can cover them, what care does she take in turning them frequently, that all parts may partake of the vital warmth? When she leaves them, to provide for her necessary sustenance, how punctually does she return before they have time to cool, and become incapable of producing an animal? In the summer you see her giving herself greater freedoms, and quitting her care for above two hours to-gether; but in winter, when the rigor of the season would chill the principles of life, and destroy the young one, she grows more assiduous in her attendance, and stays away but half the time. When the birth approaches, with how much nicety and attention does she help the chick to break its prison? Not to take notice of her covering it from the injuries of the weather, providing it proper nourishment, and teaching it to help itself; nor to mention her forsaking the nest, if after the usual time of reckoning the young one does not make its appearance. A chemical operation could not be followed with greater art or diligence, than is seen in the hatching of a chick; though there are many other birds that show an infinitely greater sagacity in all the forementioned particulars.

But at the same time the hen, that has all this seeming ingenuity, (which is indeed absolutely necessary for the propagation of the species) considered in other respects, is without the least glimmerings of thought or common sense. She mistakes a piece of chalk for an egg, and sits upon it in the same manner: she is insensible of any increase or diminution in the number of those she lays: she does not distinguish between her own and those of another species; and when the birth appears of never so different a bird, will cherish it for her own. In all these circumstances which do not carry an immediate regard to the subsistence of herself or her species, she is a very idiot.

There is not, in my opinion, anything more mysterious in nature than this instinct in animals, which thus rises above reason, and falls infinitely short of it. It cannot be accounted for by any properties in matter, and at the same time works after so odd a manner, that one cannot think it the faculty of an intellectual being. For my own part, I look upon it as upon the principle of gravitation in bodies, which is not to be explained by any known qualities inherent in the bodies themselves, nor from any laws of mechanism, but, according to the best notions of the greatest philosophers, is an immediate impression from the first Mover, and the Divine Energy acting in the creatures.

L.

THE ADAPTATION OF ANIMALS.

[*ADDISON, in* SPECTATOR, *No. 121.   Thursday, July 19, 1711.*]

"*Jovis omnia plena.*" [1]
VIRGIL, Eclogues, iii. 60.

A S I was walking this morning in the great yard that belongs
to my friend's country house, I was wonderfully pleased to
see the different workings of instinct in a hen followed by a
brood of ducks.   The young, upon the sight of a pond, immediately ran into it; while the stepmother, with all imaginable
anxiety, hovered about the borders of it, to call them out of an
element that appeared to her so dangerous and destructive.   As
the different principle which acted in these different animals cannot be termed reason, so when we call it instinct, we mean something we have no knowledge of.   To me, as I hinted in my last
paper, it seems the immediate direction of Providence, and such
an operation of the Supreme Being, as that which determines all
the portions of matter to their proper centers.   A modern philosopher, quoted by Monsieur Bayle [2] in his learned "Dissertation
on the Souls of Brutes," delivers the same opinion, though in a
bolder form of words, where he says, *Deus est anima brutorum*,
"God himself is the soul of brutes."   Who can tell what to call
that seeming sagacity in animals, which directs them to such
food as is proper for them, and makes them naturally avoid whatever is noxious or unwholesome?   Dampier, [3] in his "Travels,"

---

[1] " All things are full of Jove."
[2] Pierre Bayle (1647–1706) was a French skeptic, logician, and critic, and
one of the most independent thinkers and writers of the seventeenth century.
His principal work is an Historical and Critical Dictionary, a work of wide
learning and acuteness.
[3] William Dampier (1652–1712) was a daring English navigator who published an account of his filibustering in the West Indies, and also of his voy-
ages to the South Seas.

tells us, that when seamen are thrown upon any of the unknown coasts of America, they never venture upon the fruit of any tree, how tempting soever it may appear, unless they observe that it is marked with the pecking of birds; but fall on without any fear or apprehension where the birds have been before them.

But notwithstanding animals have nothing like the use of reason, we find in them all the lower parts of our nature, the passions and senses in their greatest strength and perfection. And here it is worth our observation, that all beasts and birds of prey are wonderfully subject to anger, malice, revenge, and all the other violent passions that may animate them in search of their proper food; as those that are incapable of defending themselves, or annoying others, or whose safety lies chiefly in their flight, are suspicious, fearful and apprehensive of everything they see or hear; whilst others that are of assistance and use to man, have their natures softened with something mild and tractable, and by that means are qualified for a domestic life. In this case the passions generally correspond with the make of the body. We do not find the fury of a lion in so weak and defenseless an animal as a lamb, nor the meekness of a lamb in a creature so armed for battle and assault as the lion. In the same manner, we find that particular animals have a more or less exquisite sharpness and sagacity in those particular senses which most turn to their advantage, and in which their safety and welfare is the most concerned.

Nor must we here omit that great variety of arms with which Nature has differently fortified the bodies of several kind of animals, such as claws, hoofs, and horns, teeth, and tusks, a tail, a sting, a trunk, or a proboscis. It is likewise observed by naturalists, that it must be some hidden principle distinct from what we call reason, which instructs animals in the use of these their arms, and teaches them to manage them to the best advantage; because they naturally defend themselves with that part in which their strength lies, before the weapon be formed in it; as is remarkable in lambs, which though they are bred within doors, and never saw the actions of their own species, push at those who approach them with their foreheads, before the first budding of a horn appears.

I shall add to these general observations, an instance which Mr. Locke[1] has given us of Providence even in the imperfections of a creature which seems the meanest and most despicable in the whole animal world. "We may," says he, "from the make of an oyster, or cockle, conclude, that it has not so many nor so quick senses as a man, or several other animals: nor if it had, would it, in that state and incapacity of transferring itself from one place to another, be bettered by them. What good would sight and hearing do to a creature, that cannot move itself to, or from the object, wherein at a distance it perceives good or evil? And would not quickness of sensation be an inconvenience to an animal, that must be still where chance has once placed it; and there receive the afflux of colder or warmer, clean or foul water, as it happens to come to it?"

I shall add to this instance out of Mr. Locke another out of the learned Dr. More,[2] who cites it from Cardan,[3] in relation to another animal which Providence has left defective, but at the same time has shown its wisdom in the formation of that organ in which it seems chiefly to have failed. "What is more obvious and ordinary than a mole? and yet what more palpable argument of Providence than she? The members of her body are so exactly fitted to her nature and manner of life: for her dwelling being under ground where nothing is to be seen, Nature has so obscurely fitted her with eyes, that naturalists can hardly agree whether she have any sight at all or no. But for amends, what she is capable of for her defense and warning of danger, she has

---

[1] See note, p. 44.

[2] Henry More (1614–87) was an eminent English divine and philosophic writer.

[3] Jerome Cardan or Cardano (1501–76) was an Italian physician, mathematician, and astrologer, one of the most interesting personages connected with the revival of science in Europe.

very eminently conferred upon her; for she is exceeding quick of hearing. And then her short tail and short legs, but broad fore feet armed with sharp claws, we see by the event to what purpose they are, she so swiftly working herself under ground, and making her way so fast in the earth as they that behold it cannot but admire it. Her legs therefore are short, that she need dig no more than will serve the mere thickness of her body; and her fore feet are broad that she may scoop away much earth at a time; and little or no tail she has, because she courses it not on the ground, like the rat or mouse, of whose kindred she is, but lives under the earth, and is fain to dig herself a dwelling there. And she making her way through so thick an element, which will not yield easily, as the air or the water, it had been dangerous to have drawn so long a train behind her; for her enemy might fall upon her rear, and fetch her out, before she had completed or got full possession of her works."

I cannot forbear mentioning Mr. Boyle's[1] remark upon this last creature, who I remember somewhere in his works observes, that though the mole be not totally blind (as it is commonly thought) she has not sight enough to distinguish particular objects. Her eye is said to have but one humor in it, which is supposed to give her the idea of light, but of nothing else, and is so formed that this idea is probably painful to the animal. Whenever she comes up into broad day she might be in danger of being taken, unless she were thus affected by a light striking upon her eye, and immediately warning her to bury herself in her proper element. More sight would be useless to her, as none at all might be fatal.

I have only instanced such animals as seem the most imperfect works of nature; and if Providence shows itself even in the blemishes of these creatures, how much more does it discover it-

[1] Robert Boyle (1626–91), often called the "Great Christian Philosopher," was a celebrated chemist and experimental philosopher, one of the founders of the Royal Society of London, and author of many learned works. He was born in Ireland.

self in the several endowments which it has variously bestowed upon such creatures as are more or less finished and completed in their several faculties, according to the condition of life in which they are posted.

I could wish our Royal Society[1] would compile a body of natural history, the best that could be gathered together from books and observations. If the several writers among them took each his particular species, and gave us a distinct account of its original, birth and education; its policies, hostilities and alliances, with the frame and texture of its inward and outward parts, and particularly those that distinguish it from all other animals, with their peculiar aptitudes for the state of being in which Providence has placed them, it would be one of the best services their studies could do mankind, and not a little redound to the glory of the all-wise Contriver.

It is true, such a natural history, after all the disquisitions of the learned, would be infinitely short and defective. Seas and deserts hide millions of animals from our observation. Innumerable artifices and stratagems are acted in the "howling wilderness" and in the "great deep," that can never come to our knowledge. Besides that there are infinitely more species of creatures which are not to be seen without, nor indeed with the help of the finest glasses, than of such as are bulky enough for the naked eye to take hold of. However from the consideration of such animals as lie within the compass of our knowledge, we might easily form a conclusion of the rest, that the same variety of wisdom and goodness runs through the whole creation, and puts every creature in a condition to provide for its safety and subsistence in its proper station.

Tully[2] has given us an admirable sketch of natural history, in his second book concerning the nature of the gods; and then in

[1] A most famous scientific society of London, founded in 1660, for the promotion of mathematical and physical science. It has included among its members most of the great men of science in England.

[2] See Note 5, p. 20.

a style so raised by metaphors and descriptions, that it lifts the subject above raillery and ridicule, which frequently fall on such nice observations when they pass through the hands of an ordinary writer. L.

SIR ROGER AMONG HIS NEIGHBORS.

[*ADDISON, in SPECTATOR, No. 122. Friday, July 20, 1711.*]

"*Comes jucundus in via pro vehiculo est.*" [1]
PUBLIUS SYRUS, Fragmenta.

A MAN'S first care should be to avoid the reproaches of his own heart; his next, to escape the censures of the world: if the last interferes with the former, it ought to be entirely neglected; but otherwise, there cannot be a greater satisfaction to an honest mind, than to see those approbations which it gives itself seconded by the applauses of the public: a man is more sure of his conduct, when the verdict which he passes upon his own behavior is thus warranted and confirmed by the opinion of all that know him.

My worthy friend Sir Roger is one of those who is not only at peace within himself, but beloved and esteemed by all about him. He receives a suitable tribute for his universal benevolence to mankind, in the returns of affection and good will, which are paid him by every one that lives within his neighborhood. I lately met with two or three odd instances of that general respect which is shown to the good old knight. He would needs carry Will Wimble and myself with him to the county assizes: [2] as we were upon the road Will Wimble joined a couple of plain men who rid before us, and conversed with them for some time; during which my friend Sir Roger acquainted me with their characters.

[1] " An agreeable companion upon the road is as good as a coach."
[2] See note, p. 52.

"The first of them," says he, "that has a spaniel by his side, is a yeoman of about a hundred pounds a year, an honest man: he is just within the Game Act,[1] and qualified to kill a hare or a pheasant: he knocks down a dinner with his gun twice or thrice a week; and by that means lives much cheaper than those who have not so good an estate as himself. He would be a good neighbor if he did not destroy so many partridges: in short, he is a very sensible man; shoots flying; and has been several times foreman of the petty jury.

"The other that rides along with him is Tom Touchy, a fellow famous for 'taking the law' of everybody. There is not one in the town where he lives that he has not sued at a quarter-sessions. The rogue had once the impudence to go to law with the widow. His head is full of costs, damages, and ejectments: he plagued a couple of honest gentlemen so long for a trespass in breaking one of his hedges, till he was forced to sell the ground it inclosed to defray the charges of the prosecution: his father left him fourscore pounds a year; but he has cast[2] and been cast so often, that he is not now worth thirty. I suppose he is going upon the old business of the Willow Tree."

As Sir Roger was giving me this account of Tom Touchy, Will Wimble and his two companions stopped short till we came up to them. After having paid their respects to Sir Roger, Will told him that Mr. Touchy and he must appeal to him upon a dispute that arose between them. Will it seems had been giving his fellow-traveler an account of his angling one day in such a hole; when Tom Touchy, instead of hearing out his story, told him that Mr. Such-a-one, if he pleased, might "take the law of him" for fishing in that part of the river. My friend Sir Roger heard them both, upon a round trot; and after having paused some

---

[1] "Just within the Game Act:" It was necessary for an Englishman to own property to the amount of a hundred pounds per annum before he was free to shoot game. A poorer man who shot a hare was a malefactor. This law was only repealed in 1827.

[2] To defeat in a lawsuit.

time told them, with the air of a man who would not give his judgment rashly, that much might be said on both sides. They were neither of them dissatisfied with the knight's determination, because neither of them found himself in the wrong by it: upon which we made the best of our way to the assizes.

The court was sat before Sir Roger came; but notwithstanding all the justices had taken their places upon the bench, they made room for the old knight at the head of them; who for his reputation in the country took occasion to whisper in the judge's ear, that he was glad his lordship had met with so much good weather in his circuit. I was listening to the proceeding of the court with much attention, and infinitely pleased with that great appearance and solemnity which so properly accompanies such a public administration of our laws; when, after about an hour's sitting, I observed to my great surprise, in the midst of a trial, that my friend Sir Roger was getting up to speak. I was in some pain for him, till I found he had acquitted himself of two or three sentences, with a look of much business and great intrepidity.

Upon his first rising the court was hushed, and a general whisper ran among the country people that Sir Roger "was up." The speech he made was so little to the purpose, that I shall not trouble my readers with an account of it; and I believe was not so much designed by the knight himself to inform the court, as to give him a figure in my eye, and keep up his credit in the country.

I was highly delighted, when the court rose, to see the gentlemen of the country gathering about my old friend, and striving who should compliment him most; at the same time that the ordinary people gazed upon him at a distance, not a little admiring his courage, that was not afraid to speak to the judge.

In our return home we met with a very odd accident; which I cannot forbear relating, because it shows how desirous all who know Sir Roger are of giving him marks of their esteem. When we were arrived upon the verge of his estate, we stopped at a

little inn to rest ourselves and our horses.   The man of the house
had it seems been formerly a servant in the knight's family; and
to do honor to his old master, had some time since, unknown to
Sir Roger, put him up in a sign-post before the door; so that the
knight's head had hung out upon the road about a week before
he himself knew anything of the matter.   As soon as Sir Roger
was acquainted with it, finding that his servant's indiscretion
proceeded wholly from affection and good will, he only told him
that he had made him too high a compliment; and when the
fellow seemed to think that could hardly be, added with a more
decisive look, that it was too great an honor for any man under
a duke; but told him at the same time, that it might be altered
with a very few touches, and that he himself would be at the
charge of it.   Accordingly they got a painter by the knight's
directions to add a pair of whiskers to the face, and by a little
aggravation to the features to change it into the Saracen's head.
I should not have known this story had not the innkeeper, upon
Sir Roger's alighting, told him in my hearing, that his honor's head
was brought back last night with the alterations that he had ordered
to be made in it.   Upon this my friend with his usual cheerfulness related the particulars above mentioned, and ordered the
head to be brought into the room.   I could not forbear discover-
ing greater expressions of mirth than ordinary upon the appearance of this monstrous face, under which, notwithstanding it was
made to frown and stare in a most extraordinary manner, I could
still discover a distant resemblance of my old friend.   Sir Roger,
upon seeing me laugh, desired me to tell him truly if I thought
it possible for people to know him in that disguise.   I at first
kept my usual silence; but upon the knight's conjuring me to
tell him whether it was not still more like himself than a Saracen,
I composed my countenance in the best manner I could, and
replied, that much might be said on both sides.

These several adventures, with the knight's behavior in them,
gave me as pleasant a day as ever I met with in any of my
travels.   L.

THE STORY OF FLORIO AND LEONILLA.

[*ADDISON, in SPECTATOR, No. 123. Saturday, July 21, 1711.*]

> "*Doctrina sed vim promovet insitam,*
> *Rectique cultus pectora roborant:*
> *Utcunque defecere mores,*
> *Dedecorant bene nata culpæ.*" [1]
> HORACE, Lib. IV., Ode iv. 33.

AS I was yesterday taking the air with my friend Sir Roger, we were met by a fresh-colored ruddy young man, who rid by us full speed, with a couple of servants behind him. Upon my inquiry who he was, Sir Roger told me that he was a young gentleman of a considerable estate, who had been educated by a tender mother that lives not many miles from the place where we were. She is a very good lady, says my friend, but took so much care of her son's health, that she has made him good for nothing. She quickly found that reading was bad for his eyes, and that writing made his head ache. He was let loose among the woods as soon as he was able to ride on horseback, or to carry a gun upon his shoulder. To be brief, I found, by my friend's account of him, that he had got a great stock of health, but nothing else; and that if it were a man's business only to live, there would not be a more accomplished young fellow in the whole country.

The truth of it is, since my residing in these parts I have seen and heard innumerable instances of young heirs and elder brothers, who either from their own reflecting upon the estates they are born to, and therefore thinking all other accomplishments unnecessary, or from hearing these notions frequently in-

---

[1] Oldisworth's translation: —

> "Yet the best blood by learning is refin'd,
> And virtue arms the solid mind;
>   Whilst vice will stain the noblest race,
>   And the paternal stamp efface."

culcated to them by the flattery of their servants and domestics, or from the same foolish thought prevailing in those who have the care of their education, are of no manner of use but to keep up their families, and transmit their lands and houses in a line to posterity.

This makes me often think on a story I have heard of two friends, which I shall give my reader at large, under feigned names. The moral of it may, I hope, be useful, though there are some circumstances which make it rather appear like a novel, than a true story.

Eudoxus and Leontine began the world with small estates. They were both of them men of good sense and great virtue. They prosecuted their studies together in their earlier years, and entered into such a friendship as lasted to the end of their lives. Eudoxus, at his first setting out in the world, threw himself into a court, where by his natural endowments and his acquired abilities he made his way from one post to another, till at length he had raised a very considerable fortune. Leontine on the contrary sought all opportunities of improving his mind by study, conversation, and travel. He was not only acquainted with all the sciences, but with the most eminent professors of them throughout Europe. He knew perfectly well the interests of its princes, with the customs and fashions of their courts, and could scarce meet with the name of an extraordinary person in the "Gazette" whom he had not either talked to or seen. In short, he had so well mixed and digested his knowledge of men and books, that he made one of the most accomplished persons of his age. During the whole course of his studies and travels he kept up a punctual correspondence with Eudoxus, who often made himself acceptable to the principal men about court by the intelligence which he received from Leontine. When they were both turned of forty (an age in which, according to Mr. Cowley, "there is no dallying with life") they determined, pursuant to the resolution they had taken in the beginning of their lives, to retire, and pass the remainder of their days in the country. In order to this, they both of them married much about the same time. Leontine, with his own and his wife's fortune, bought a farm of three hundred a year, which lay within the neighborhood of his friend Eudoxus, who had purchased an estate of as many thousands. They were both of them fathers about the same time, Eudoxus having a son born to him, and Leontine a daughter; but to the unspeakable grief of the latter, his young wife (in whom all his happiness was wrapped up) died in a few days after the birth of her daughter. His affliction would have been insupportable, had not he been comforted by the daily visits and conversations of his friend. As they were one day talking together with their usual intimacy, Leontine, considering how incapable he was of giving his daughter a proper education in his own house, and Eudoxus reflecting on the ordinary behavior of a son who knows himself to be the heir of a great estate, they both agreed upon an exchange of children, namely that the boy should be bred up with Leontine as his son, and that the girl should live with Eudoxus as his daughter, till they were each of them arrived at years of discretion. The wife of Eudoxus, knowing that her son could not be so advantageously brought up as under the care of Leontine, and considering at the same time that he would be perpetually under her own eye, was by degrees prevailed upon to fall in with the project. She therefore took Leonilla, for that was the name of the girl, and educated her as her own daughter. The two friends on each side had wrought themselves to such an habitual tenderness for the children who were under their direction, that each of them had the real passion of a father, where the title was but imaginary. Florio, the name of the young heir that lived with Leontine, though he had all the duty and affection imaginable for his supposed parent, was taught to rejoice at the sight of Eudoxus, who visited his friend very frequently, and was dictated by his natural affection, as well as by the rules of prudence, to make himself esteemed and beloved by Florio. The boy was now old enough to know his supposed father's circumstances, and that therefore he was to make his way in the world by his own industry. This consideration grew stronger in him every day, and produced so good an effect, that he applied himself with more than ordinary attention to the pursuit of everything which Leontine recommended to him. His natural abilities, which were very good, assisted by the directions of so excellent a counselor, enabled him to make a quicker progress than ordinary through all the parts of his education. Before he was twenty years of age, having finished his studies and exercises with great applause, he was removed from the university to the inns of court, where there are very few that make themselves considerable proficients in the studies of the place, who know they shall arrive at great estates without them. This was not Florio's case; he found that three hundred a year was but a poor estate for Leontine and himself to live upon, so that he studied without intermission till he gained a very good insight into the constitution and laws of his country.

I should have told my reader, that whilst Florio lived at the house of his foster father, he was always an acceptable guest in the family of Eudoxus, where he became acquainted with Leonilla from her infancy. His acquaintance with her by degrees grew into love, which in a mind trained up in all the sentiments of honor and virtue became a very uneasy passion. He despaired of gaining an heiress of so great a fortune, and would rather have died than attempted it by any indirect methods. Leonilla, who was a woman of the greatest beauty joined with the greatest modesty, entertained at the same time a secret passion for Florio, but conducted herself with so much prudence that she never gave him the least intimation of it. Florio was now engaged in all those arts and improvements that are proper to raise a man's private fortune, and give him a figure in his country, but secretly tormented with that passion which burns with the greatest fury in a virtuous and noble heart, when he received a sudden summons from Leontine, to repair to him into the country the next day. For it seems Eudoxus was so filled with the report of his son's reputation, that he could no longer withhold making himself known to him. The morning after his arrival at the house of his supposed father, Leontine told him that Eudoxus had something of great importance to communicate to him; upon which the good man embraced him, and wept. Florio was no sooner arrived at the great house that stood in his neighborhood, but Eudoxus took him by the hand, after the first salutes were over, and conducted him into his closet. He there opened to him the whole secret of his parentage and education, concluding after this manner: "I have no other way left of acknowledging my gratitude to Leontine, than by marrying you to his daughter. He shall not lose the pleasure of being your father by the discovery I have made to you. Leonilla too shall be still my daughter; her filial piety, though misplaced, has been so exemplary that it deserves the greatest reward I can confer upon it. You shall have the pleasure of seeing a great estate fall to you, which you would have lost the relish of had you known yourself born to it. Continue only to deserve it in the same manner you did before you were possessed of it. I have left your mother in the next room. Her heart yearns towards you. She is making the same discoveries to Leonilla which I have made to yourself." Florio was so overwhelmed with this profusion of happiness, that he was not able to make a reply, but threw himself down at his father's feet, and amidst a flood of tears, kissed and embraced his knees, asking his blessing, and expressing in dumb show those sentiments of love, duty, and gratitude that were too big for utterance. To conclude, the happy pair were married, and half Eudoxus's estate settled upon them. Leontine and Eudoxus passed the remainder of their lives together; and received in the dutiful and affectionate behavior of Florio and Leonilla the just recompense, as well as the natural effects of that care which they had bestowed upon them in their education.   L.

PARTY SPIRIT.

[*ADDISON, in* SPECTATOR, *No. 125.   Tuesday, July 24, 1711.*]

> "*Ne pueri, ne tanta animis assuescite bella :
> Neu patriæ validas in viscera vertite vires.*" [1]
>
> VIRGIL, Æneid, Lib. VI. 832.

MY worthy friend Sir Roger, when we are talking of the malice of parties, very frequently tells us an accident that happened to him when he was a schoolboy, which was at a time when the feuds ran high between the Roundheads and Cavaliers.[2] This worthy knight, being then but a stripling, had occasion to inquire which was the way to St. Anne's Lane, upon which the person whom he spoke to, instead of answering his question, called him a young popish cur, and asked him who had made Anne a saint?   The boy, being in some confusion, inquired of the next he met, which was the way to Anne's Lane ; but was called a prick-eared cur for his pains, and instead of being shown the way, was told that she had been a saint before he was born, and would be one after he was hanged.   "Upon this," says Sir Roger, "I did not think fit to repeat the former question, but going into every lane of the neighborhood, asked what they called the name of that lane."   By which ingenious artifice he found out the place he inquired after, without giving offense to any party.   Sir Roger generally closes this narrative with reflections on the mischief that parties do in the country ; how they spoil good neighborhood, and make honest gentlemen hate one an-

---

[1] Dryden's translation : —

> "This thirst of kindred blood, my sons, detest,
>   Nor turn your face against your country's breast."

[2] "Roundheads" was the name given to the English Parliamentary party in the reign of Charles I.   It was composed mostly of Puritans, who wore their hair cut short.   The Cavaliers composed the Royalist party, were mostly Catholics, and wore their hair in long ringlets.

other; besides that they manifestly tend to the prejudice of the land-tax, and the destruction of the game.

There cannot a greater judgment befall a country than such a dreadful spirit of division as rends a government into two distinct people, and makes them greater strangers and more averse to one another, than if they were actually two different nations. The effects of such a division are pernicious to the last degree, not only with regard to those advantages which they give the common enemy, but to those private evils which they produce in the heart of almost every particular person. This influence is very fatal both to men's morals and their understandings; it sinks the virtue of a nation, and not only so, but destroys even common sense.

A furious party spirit, when it rages in its full violence, exerts itself in civil war and bloodshed; and when it is under its greatest restraints naturally breaks out in falsehood, detraction, calumny, and a partial administration of justice. In a word, it fills a nation with spleen and rancor, and extinguishes all the seeds of good nature, compassion and humanity.

Plutarch[1] says very finely, that a man should not allow himself to hate even his enemies, "because," says he, "if you indulge this passion in some occasions, it will rise of itself in others; if you hate your enemies, you will contract such a vicious habit of mind, as by degrees will break out upon those who are your friends, or those who are indifferent to you." I might here observe how admirably this precept of morality (which derives the malignity of hatred from the passion itself, and not from its object) answers to that great rule[2] which was dictated to the world about a hundred years before this philosopher wrote; but in-

---

[1] Plutarch (born about A.D. 50, date of death unknown), a great Greek philosopher and moralist, was the most famous biographer of antiquity. His Lives of the Greeks and Romans is admired and read wherever letters are known.

[2] " Love your enemies, do good to them which hate you, bless them that curse you," etc. (Luke vi. 27-32).

stead of that, I shall only take notice, with a real grief of heart, that the minds of many good men among us appear soured with party principles, and alienated from one another in such a manner, as seems to me altogether inconsistent with the dictates either of reason or religion. Zeal for a public cause is apt to breed passions in the hearts of virtuous persons, to which the regard of their own private interest would never have betrayed them.

If this party spirit has so ill an effect on our morals, it has likewise a very great one upon our judgments. We often hear a poor insipid paper or pamphlet cried up, and sometimes a noble piece depreciated, by those who are of a different principle from the author. One who is actuated by this spirit is almost under an incapacity of discerning either real blemishes or beauties. A man of merit in a different principle, is like an object seen in two different mediums, ·that appears crooked or broken, however straight and entire it may be in itself. For this reason there is scarce a person of any figure in England, who does not go by two contrary characters, as opposite to one another as light and darkness. Knowledge and learning suffer in a particular manner from this strange prejudice, which at present prevails amongst all ranks and degrees in the British nation. As men formerly became eminent in learned societies by their parts and acquisitions, they now distinguish themselves by the warmth and violence with which they espouse their respective parties. Books are valued upon the like considerations: an abusive scurrilous style passes for satire, and a dull scheme of party notions is called fine writing.

There is one piece of sophistry practiced by both sides, and that is the taking any scandalous story that has been ever whispered or invented of a private man, for a known undoubted truth, and raising suitable speculations upon it. Calumnies that have been never proved, or have been often refuted, are the ordinary postulatums of these infamous scribblers, upon which they proceed as upon first principles granted by all men, though in their hearts they know they are false, or at best very doubtful. When they have laid these foundations of scurrility, it is no wonder that their superstructure is every way answerable to them. If this shameless practice of the present age endures much longer, praise and reproach will cease to be motives of action in good men.

There are certain periods of time in all governments when this inhuman spirit prevails. Italy was long torn in pieces by the Guelphs and Ghibellines,[1] and France by those who were for and against the League:[2] but it is very unhappy for a man to be born in such a stormy and tempestuous season. It is the restless ambition of artful men that thus breaks a people into factions, and draws several well-meaning persons to their interest by a specious concern for their country. How many honest minds are filled with uncharitable and barbarous notions, out of their zeal for the public good? What cruelties and outrages would they not commit against men of an adverse party, whom they would honor and esteem, if instead of considering them as they are represented, they knew them as they are? Thus are persons of the greatest probity seduced into shameful errors and prejudices, and made bad men even by that noblest of principles, the love of their country. I cannot here forbear mentioning the famous Spanish proverb, "If there were neither fools nor knaves in the world, all people would be of one mind."

For my own part, I could heartily wish that all honest men would enter into an association, for the support of one another against the endeavors of those whom they ought to look upon as their common enemies, whatsoever side they may belong to. Were there such an honest body of neutral forces, we should never see the worst of men in great figures of life, because they are

---

[1] The Guelphs and Ghibellines were originally two famous families in the twelfth century. The Guelphs represented the Pope's party; and the Ghibellines, the imperial or civil party. "Ghibellines" was a name afterwards applied to Italian rebels; and "Guelphs," that applied to the government party of Italy.

[2] The Catholic League formed by the Duke of Guise to insure Catholic succession for the crown of Henry III. of France (1576).

useful to a party; nor the best unregarded, because they are above practicing those methods which would be grateful to their faction. We should then single every criminal out of the herd, and hunt him down, however formidable and overgrown he might appear: on the contrary, we should shelter distressed innocence, and defend virtue, however beset with contempt or ridicule, envy or defamation. In short, we should not any longer regard our fellow-subjects as Whigs or Tories, but should make the man of merit our friend, and the villain our enemy.

C.

POLITICAL DISSENSIONS.

[*ADDISON, in* SPECTATOR, *No. 126. Wednesday, July 25, 1711.*]

"Tros Rutulusve fuat, nullo discrimine habebo." [1]
VIRGIL, Æneid, Lib. X. 108.

IN my yesterday's paper I proposed, that the honest men of all parties should enter into a kind of association for the defense of one another, and the confusion of their common enemies. As it is designed this neutral body should act with a regard to nothing but truth and equity, and divest themselves of the little heats and prepossessions that cleave to parties of all kinds, I have prepared for them the following form of an association, which may express their intentions in the most plain and simple manner.

"We whose names are hereunto subscribed do solemnly declare, that we do in our consciences believe two and two make four; and that we shall adjudge any man whatsoever to be our enemy who endeavors to persuade us to the contrary. We are likewise ready to maintain, with the hazard of all that is near and dear to us, that six is less than seven in all times and all places; and that ten will not be more three years hence than it is at present. We do also firmly declare, that it is our resolution as long as we live to call black black, and white white. And we shall upon all occasions oppose such

1 "Rutulians, Trojans, are the same to me."

persons that upon any day of the year shall call black white, or white black, with the utmost peril of our lives and fortunes."

Were there such a combination of honest men, who without any regard to places would endeavor to extirpate all such furious zealots as would sacrifice one half of their country to the passion and interest of the other; as also such infamous hypocrites, that are for promoting their own advantage, under color of the public good; with all the profligate immoral retainers to each side, that have nothing to recommend them but an implicit submission to their leaders; we should soon see that furious party spirit extinguished, which may in time expose us to the derision and contempt of all the nations about us.

A member of this society, that would thus carefully employ himself in making room for merit, by throwing down the worthless and depraved part of mankind from those conspicuous stations of life to which they have been sometimes advanced, and all this without any regard to his private interest, would be no small benefactor to his country.

I remember to have read in Diodorus Siculus[1] an account of a very active little animal, which I think he calls the ichneumon, that makes it the whole business of his life to break the eggs of the crocodile, which he is always in search after. This instinct is the more remarkable, because the ichneumon never feeds upon the eggs he has broken, nor in any other way finds his account in them. Were it not for the incessant labors of this industrious animal, Egypt, says the historian, would be overrun with crocodiles; for the Egyptians are so far from destroying those pernicious creatures, that they worship them as gods.

If we look into the behavior of ordinary partisans, we shall find them far from resembling this disinterested animal; and rather acting after the example of the wild Tartars, who are ambitious of destroying a man of the most extraordinary parts and

[1] Diodorus Siculus (born in the first century before Christ) was an eminent Greek writer and historian. He wrote a history of the world, in forty books, only fifteen of which have been preserved.

accomplishments, as thinking that upon his decease the same talents, whatever post they qualified him for, enter of course into his destroyer.

As in the whole train of my speculations, I have endeavored as much as I am able to extinguish that pernicious spirit of passion and prejudice, which rages with the same violence in all parties, I am still the more desirous of doing some good in this particular, because I observe that the spirit of party reigns more in the country than in the town. It here contracts a kind of brutality and rustic fierceness, to which men of a politer conversation are wholly strangers. It extends itself even to the return of the bow and the hat; and at the same time that the heads of parties preserve towards one another an outward show of good breeding, and keep up a perpetual intercourse of civilities, their tools that are dispersed in these outlying parts will not so much as mingle together at a cock-match. This humor fills the country with several periodical meetings of Whig jockeys and Tory fox-hunters; not to mention the innumerable curses, frowns, and whispers it produces at a quarter-sessions.

I do not know whether I have observed in any of my former papers, that my friends Sir Roger de Coverley and Sir Andrew Freeport are of different principles, the first of them inclined to the landed and the other to the moneyed interest. This humor is so moderate in each of them, that it proceeds no further than to an agreeable raillery, which very often diverts the rest of the Club. I find however that the knight is a much stronger Tory in the country than in town, which, as he has told me in my ear, is absolutely necessary for the keeping-up his interest. In all our journey from London to his house we did not so much as bait at a Whig inn; or if by chance the coachman stopped at a wrong place, one of Sir Roger's servants would ride up to his master full speed, and whisper to him that the master of the house was against such a one in the last election. This often betrayed us into hard beds and bad cheer; for we were not so inquisitive about the inn as the innkeeper; and, provided our landlord's principles were sound, did not take any notice of the staleness of his provisions. This I found still the more inconvenient, because the better the host was, the worse generally were his accommodations; the fellow knowing very well, that those who were his friends would take up with coarse diet and a hard lodging. For these reasons, all the while I was upon the road I dreaded entering into a house of any one that Sir Roger had applauded for an honest man.

Since my stay at Sir Roger's in the country, I daily find more instances of this narrow party humor. Being upon a bowling-green[1] at a neighboring market town the other day, (for that is the place where the gentlemen of one side meet once a week) I observed a stranger among them of a better presence and genteeler behavior than ordinary; but was much surprised, that notwithstanding he was a very fair better, nobody would take him up. But upon inquiry I found, that he was one who had given a disagreeable vote in a former Parliament, for which reason there was not a man upon that bowling-green who would have so much correspondence with him as to win his money of him.

Among other instances of this nature, I must not omit one which concerns myself. Will Wimble was the other day relating several strange stories that he had picked up nobody knows where of a certain great man; and upon my staring at him, as one that was surprised to hear such things in the country which had never been so much as whispered in the town, Will stopped short in the thread of his discourse, and after dinner asked my friend Sir Roger in his ear if he was sure that I was not a fanatic.

It gives me a serious concern to see such a spirit of dissension in the country; not only as it destroys virtue and common sense, and renders us in a manner barbarians towards one another, but as it perpetuates our animosities, widens our breaches, and transmits our present passions and prejudices to our posterity. For

[1] A level piece of greensward or smooth ground for bowling, — a game known in England as early as the thirteenth century.

my own part, I am sometimes afraid that I discover the seeds of a civil war in these our divisions; and therefore cannot but bewail, as in their first principles, the miseries and calamities of our children.   C.

SIR ROGER AND THE GYPSIES.

[*ADDISON, in SPECTATOR, No. 130.   Monday, July 30, 1711.*]

"Semperque recentes
Convectare juvat prædas, et vivere rapto." [1]
VIRGIL, Æneid, Lib. VII. 748.

AS I was yesterday riding out in the fields with my friend Sir Roger, we saw at a little distance from us a troop of gypsies. Upon the first discovery of them, my friend was in some doubt whether he should not exert the justice of the peace upon such a band of lawless vagrants; but not having his clerk with him, who is a necessary counselor on these occasions, and fearing that his poultry might fare the worse for it, he let the thought drop: but at the same time gave me a particular account of the mischiefs they do in the country, in stealing people's goods and spoiling their servants. "If a stray piece of linen hangs upon a hedge," says Sir Roger, "they are sure to have it; if the hog loses his way in the fields, it is ten to one but he becomes their prey; our geese cannot live in peace for them; if a man prosecutes them with severity, his hen-roost is sure to pay for it: they generally straggle into these parts about this time of the year; and set the heads of our servant-maids so agog for husbands, that we do not expect to have any business done as it should be whilst they are in the country. I have an honest dairymaid who crosses their hands with a piece of silver every summer, and never fails being promised the handsomest young fellow

---

[1] Free translation: —

          "A plundering race, still eager to invade,
            On spoil they live, and make of theft a trade."

in the parish for her pains. Your friend the butler has been fool enough to be seduced by them; and, though he is sure to lose a knife, a fork, or a spoon every time his fortune is told him, generally shuts himself up in the pantry with an old gypsy for above half an hour once in a twelvemonth. Sweethearts are the things they live upon, which they bestow very plentifully upon all those that apply themselves to them. You see now and then some handsome young jades among them: the slatterns have very often white teeth and black eyes."

Sir Roger observing that I listened with great attention to his account of a people who were so entirely new to me, told me, that if I would they should tell us our fortunes. As I was very well pleased with the knight's proposal, we rid up and communicated our hands to them. A Cassandra[1] of the crew, after having examined my lines very diligently, told me, that I loved a pretty maid in a corner, that I was a good woman's man, with some other particulars which I do not think proper to relate. My friend Sir Roger alighted from his horse, and exposing his palm to two or three that stood by him, they crumpled it into all shapes, and diligently scanned every wrinkle that could be made in it; when one of them, who was older and more sunburnt than the rest, told him, that he had a widow in his line of life: upon which the knight cried, "Go, go, you are an idle baggage;" and at the same time smiled upon me. The gypsy finding he was not displeased in his heart, told him, after a further inquiry into his hand, that his true-love was constant, and that she should dream of him to-night: my old friend cried "Pish," and bid her go on. The gypsy told him that he was a bachelor, but would not be so long; and that he was dearer to somebody than he thought: the knight still repeated, she was an idle baggage, and bid her go on. "Ah master," says the gypsy, "that roguish leer of yours makes a pretty woman's heart ache; you ha'n't that simper about the mouth for nothing"— The uncouth gibberish

---

[1] Cassandra, daughter of Priam and Hecuba, was celebrated for her prophetic powers. During the siege of Troy she predicted its downfall.

with which all this was uttered like the darkness of an oracle, made us the more attentive to it. To be short, the knight left the money with her that he had crossed her hand with, and got up again on his horse.

As we were riding away, Sir Roger told me, that he knew several sensible people who believed these gypsies now and then foretold very strange things; and for half an hour together appeared more jocund than ordinary. In the height of his good humor, meeting a common beggar upon the road who was no conjuror, as he went to relieve him he found his pocket was picked: that being a kind of palmistry at which this race of vermin are very dexterous.

I might here entertain my reader with historical remarks on this idle profligate people, who infest all the countries of Europe, and live in the midst of governments in a kind of commonwealth by themselves. But instead of entering into observations of this nature, I shall fill the remaining part of my paper with a story which is still fresh in Holland, and was printed in one of our monthly accounts about twenty years ago. "As the *trekschuyt*, or hackney-boat, which carries passengers from Leyden to Amsterdam, was putting off, a boy running along the side of the canal desired to be taken in; which the master of the boat refused, because the lad had not quite money enough to pay the usual fare. An eminent merchant being pleased with the looks of the boy, and secretly touched with compassion towards him, paid the money for him, and ordered him to be taken on board. Upon talking with him afterwards, he found that he could speak readily in three or four languages, and learned upon further examination that he had been stolen away when he was a child by a gypsy, and had rambled ever since with a gang of those strollers up and down several parts of Europe. It happened that the merchant, whose heart seems to have inclined towards the boy by a secret kind of instinct, had himself lost a child some years before. The parents, after a long search for him, gave him for drowned in one of the canals with which that country abounds; and the mother was so afflicted at the loss of a fine boy, who was her only son, that she died for grief of it. Upon laying together all particulars, and examining the several moles and marks by which the mother used to describe the child when he was first missing, the boy proved to be the son of the merchant whose heart had so unaccountably melted at the sight of him. The lad was very well pleased to find a father who was so rich, and likely to leave him a good estate; the father on the other hand was not a little delighted to see a son return to him, whom he had given for lost, with such a strength of constitution, sharpness of understanding, and skill in languages." Here the printed story leaves off; but if I may give credit to reports, our linguist having received such extraordinary rudiments towards a good education, was afterwards trained up in everything that becomes a gentleman; wearing off by little and little all the vicious habits and practices that he had been used to in the course of his peregrinations: nay, it is said, that he has since been employed in foreign courts upon national business, with great reputation to himself and honor to those who sent him, and that he has visited several countries as a public minister, in which he formerly wandered as a gypsy. C.

THE SPECTATOR SUMMONED TO LONDON.

[*ADDISON, in SPECTATOR, No. 131. Tuesday, July 31, 1711.*]

"*Ipsæ rursum concedite sylvæ.*" [1]
VIRGIL, Eclogues, x. 63.

IT is usual for a man who loves country sports to preserve the game in his own grounds, and divert himself upon those that belong to his neighbor. My friend Sir Roger generally goes two or three miles from his house, and gets into the frontiers of his estate, before he beats about in search of a hare or partridge,

---

[1] " Once more, ye woods, adieu."

on purpose to spare his own fields, where he is always sure of
finding diversion, when the worst comes to the worst.   By this
means the breed about his house has time to increase and mul-
tiply, besides that the sport is the more agreeable where the
game is the harder to come at, and where it does not lie so thick
as to produce any perplexity or confusion in the pursuit.   For
these reasons the country gentleman, like the fox, seldom preys
near his own home.

   In the same manner I have made a month's excursion out of
the town, which is the great field of game for sportsmen of my
species, to try my fortune in the country, where I have started
several subjects, and hunted them down, with some pleasure to
myself, and I hope to others.   I am here forced to use a great
deal of diligence before I can spring anything to my mind,
whereas in town, whilst I am following one character, it is ten to
one but I am crossed in my way by another, and put up such a
variety of odd creatures in both sexes, that they foil the scent of
one another, and puzzle the chase.   My greatest difficulty in the
country is to find sport, and in town to choose it.   In the mean
time, as I have given a whole month's rest to the cities of London and Westminster, I promise myself abundance of new game
upon my return thither.

   It is indeed high time for me to leave the country, since I find
the whole neighborhood begin to grow very inquisitive after my
name and character.   My love of solitude, taciturnity, and particular way of life, having raised a great curiosity in all these
parts.

   The notions which have been framed of me are various; some
look upon me as very proud, some as very modest, and some as
very melancholy.   Will Wimble, as my friend the butler tells me,
observing me very much alone, and extremely silent when I am
in company, is afraid I have killed a man.   The country people
seem to suspect me for a conjurer; and some of them hearing of
the visit which I made to Moll White, will needs have it that Sir
Roger has brought down a cunning man with him, to cure the

old woman, and free the country from her charms. So that the character which I go under in part of the neighborhood, is what they here call a "white witch."

A justice of peace, who lives about five miles off, and is not of Sir Roger's party, has it seems said twice or thrice at his table, that he wishes Sir Roger does not harbor a Jesuit in his house, and that he thinks the gentlemen of the country would do very well to make me give some account of myself.

On the other side, some of Sir Roger's friends are afraid the old knight is imposed upon by a designing fellow, and as they have heard that he converses very promiscuously when he is in town, do not know but he has brought down with him some discarded Whig, that is sullen, and says nothing, because he is out of place.

Such is the variety of opinions which are here entertained of me, so that I pass among some for a disaffected person, and among others for a popish priest; among some for a wizard, and among others for a murderer; and all this for no other reason, that I can imagine, but because I do not hoot and halloo and make a noise. It is true my friend Sir Roger tells them, that it is my way, and that I am only a philosopher; but this will not satisfy them. They think there is more in me than he discovers, and that I do not hold my tongue for nothing.

For these and other reasons I shall set out for London tomorrow, having found by experience that the country is not a place for a person of my temper, who does not love jollity, and what they call good neighborhood. A man that is out of humor when an unexpected guest breaks in upon him, and does not care for sacrificing an afternoon to every chance-comer; that will be the master of his own time, and the pursuer of his own inclinations, makes but a very unsociable figure in this kind of life. I shall therefore retire into the town, if I may make use of that phrase, and get into the crowd again as fast as I can, in order to be alone. I can there raise what speculations I please upon others without being observed myself, and at the same time enjoy all the advantages of company with all the privileges of solitude. In the mean while, to finish the month and conclude these my rural speculations, I shall here insert a letter from my friend Will Honeycomb, who has not lived a month for these forty years out of the smoke of London, and rallies me after his way upon my country life.

DEAR SPEC,—I suppose this letter will find thee picking of daisies, or smelling to a lock of hay, or passing away thy time in some innocent country diversion of the like nature. I have however orders from the Club to summon thee up to town, being all of us cursedly afraid thou wilt not be able to relish our company, after thy conversations with Moll White and Will Wimble. Prithee don't send us up any more stories of a cock and a bull, nor frighten the town with spirits and witches. Thy speculations begin to smell confoundedly of woods and meadows. If thou dost not come up quickly, we shall conclude that thou art in love with one of Sir Roger's dairy-maids. Service to the knight. Sir Andrew is grown the cock of the Club since he left us, and if he does not return quickly will make every mother's son of us commonwealth's men. Dear Spec,

Thine eternally,

WILL HONEYCOMB.

C.

THE JOURNEY TO LONDON.

[*STEELE, in SPECTATOR, No. 132. Wednesday, August 1, 1711.*]

"*Qui aut tempus quid postulet non videt, aut plura loquitur, aut se ostentat, aut eorum quibuscum est rationem non habet, is ineptus esse dicitur.*" [1]

TULLY.

HAVING notified to my good friend Sir Roger that I should set out for London the next day, his horses were ready at the appointed hour in the evening; and attended by one of his grooms, I arrived at the county town at twilight, in order to be ready for the stagecoach the day following. As soon as we

---

[1] " That man may be called impertinent, who considers not the circumstances of time, or engrosses the conversation, or makes himself the subject of his discourse, or pays no regard to the company he is in."

arrived at the inn, the servant who waited upon me, inquired of the chamberlain in my hearing what company he had for the coach? The fellow answered, "Mrs. Betty Arable, the great fortune, and the widow her mother; a recruiting officer (who took a place because they were to go;) young Squire Quickset her cousin (that her mother wished her to be married to;) Ephraim the Quaker, her guardian; and a gentleman that had studied himself dumb from Sir Roger de Coverley's." I observed by what he said of myself, that according to his office he dealt much in intelligence; and doubted not but there was some foundation for his reports of the rest of the company, as well as for the whimsical account he gave of me. The next morning at daybreak we were all called; and I, who know my own natural shyness, and endeavor to be as little liable to be disputed with as possible, dressed immediately, that I might make no one wait. The first preparation for our setting-out was, that the captain's half-pike was placed near the coachman, and a drum behind the coach. In the mean time the drummer, the captain's equipage, was very loud, that none of the captain's things should be placed so as to be spoiled; upon which his cloak-bag was fixed in the seat of the coach: and the captain himself, according to a frequent, though invidious behavior of military men, ordered his man to look sharp, that none but one of the ladies should have the place he had taken fronting to the coach-box.

We were in some little time fixed in our seats, and sat with that dislike which people not too good-natured usually conceive of each other at first sight. The coach jumbled us insensibly into some sort of familiarity: and we had not moved above two miles, when the widow asked the captain what success he had in his recruiting? The officer, with a frankness he believed very graceful, told her, that indeed he had but very little luck, and had suffered much by desertion, therefore should be glad to end his warfare in the service of her or her fair daughter. "In a word," continued he, "I am a soldier, and to be plain is my character: you see me, madam, young, sound, and impudent;

take me yourself, widow, or give me to her, I will be wholly at
your disposal. I am a soldier of fortune, ha!" This was followed by a vain laugh of his own, and a deep silence of all the
rest of the company. I had nothing left for it but to fall fast
asleep, which I did with all speed. "Come," said he, "resolve
upon it, we will make a wedding at the next town: we will wake
this pleasant companion who is fallen asleep, to be the brideman,
and" (giving the Quaker a clap on the knee) he concluded,
"this sly saint, who, I'll warrant, understands what's what as well
as you or I, widow, shall give the bride as father." The Quaker,
who happened to be a man of smartness, answered, "Friend, I
take it in good part that thou hast given me the authority of a
father over this comely and virtuous child; and I must assure
thee, that if I have the giving her, I shall not bestow her on
thee. Thy mirth, friend, savoreth of folly: thou art a person of
a light mind; thy drum is a type of thee, it soundeth because it
is empty. Verily, it is not from thy fullness, but thy emptiness
that thou hast spoken this day. Friend, friend, we have hired
this coach in partnership with thee, to carry us to the great city;
we cannot go any other way. This worthy mother must hear
thee if thou wilt needs utter thy follies; we cannot help it, friend,
I say: if thou wilt we must hear thee: but if thou wert a man
of understanding, thou wouldst not take advantage of thy coura-
geous countenance to abash us children of peace. Thou art,
thou sayest, a soldier; give quarter to us, who cannot resist thee.
Why didst thou fleer at our friend, who feigned himself asleep?
he said nothing: but how dost thou know what he containeth?
If thou speakest improper things in the hearing of this virtuous
young virgin, consider it as an outrage against a distressed person
that cannot get from thee: to speak indiscreetly what we are
obliged to hear, by being hasped up with thee in this public
vehicle, is in some degree assaulting on the high road."

Here Ephraim paused, and the captain with a happy and uncommon impudence (which can be convicted and support itself
at the same time) cries, "Faith, friend, I thank thee; I should

have been a little impertinent if thou hadst not reprimanded me. Come, thou art, I see, a smoky old fellow, and I'll be very orderly the ensuing part of the journey. I was going to give myself airs, but, ladies, I beg pardon."

The captain was so little out of humor, and our company was so far from being soured by this little ruffle, that Ephraim and he took a particular delight in being agreeable to each other for the future; and assumed their different provinces in the conduct of the company. Our reckonings, apartments, and accommodation, fell under Ephraim: and the captain looked to all disputes on the road, as the good behavior of our coachman, and the right we had of taking place as going to London of all vehicles coming from thence. The occurrences we met with were ordinary, and very little happened which could entertain by the relation of them: but when I considered the company we were in, I took it for no small good fortune that the whole journey was not spent in impertinences, which to one part of us might be an entertainment, to the other a suffering. What therefore Ephraim said when we were almost arrived at London, had to me an air not only of good understanding but good breeding. Upon the young lady's expressing her satisfaction in the journey, and declaring how delightful it had been to her, Ephraim declared himself as follows: "There is no ordinary part of human life which expresseth so much a good mind, and a right inward man, as his behavior upon meeting with strangers, especially such as may seem the most unsuitable companions to him: such a man, when he falleth in the way with persons of simplicity and innocence, however knowing he may be in the ways of men, will not vaunt himself thereof; but will the rather hide his superiority to them, that he may not be painful unto them. My good friend," (continued he, turning to the officer) "thee and I are to part by and by, and peradventure we may never meet again: but be advised by a plain man; modes and apparel are but trifles to the real man, therefore do not think such a man as thyself terrible for thy garb, nor such a one as me contemptible for mine. When two such as thee and I meet, with affections as we ought to have towards each other, thou shouldst rejoice to see my peaceable demeanor, and I should be glad to see thy strength and ability to protect me in it."   T.

A DEBATE AT THE CLUB.

[STEELE, *in* SPECTATOR, *No. 174. Wednesday, September 19, 1711.*]

"Hæc memini et victum frustra contendere Thyrsin." [1]
VIRGIL, Eclogues, vii. 69.

THERE is scarce anything more common than animosities between parties that cannot subsist but by their agreement: this was well represented in the sedition of the members of the human body in the old Roman fable.[2]   It is often the case of lesser confederate states against a superior power, which are hardly held together, though their unanimity is necessary for their common safety: and this is always the case of the landed and trading interest of Great Britain: the trader is fed by the product of the land, and the landed man cannot be clothed but by the skill of the trader; and yet those interests are ever jarring.

We had last winter an instance of this at our Club, in Sir Roger de Coverley and Sir Andrew Freeport, between whom there is generally a constant, though friendly, opposition of opinions. It happened that one of the company, in an historical discourse, was observing, that "Carthaginian faith" was a proverbial phrase to intimate breach of leagues.   Sir Roger said it could hardly be otherwise: that the Carthaginians were the greatest traders in the world; and as gain is the chief end of such a people, they

---

[1] Free translation : —

" The whole debate in mem'ry I retain,
    When Thyrsis argued warmly, but in vain."

[2] Livy, History of Rome, Book II. chap. 32.

never pursue any other: the means to it are never regarded; they will, if it comes easily, get money honestly; but if not, they will not scruple to attain it by fraud or cozenage: and indeed, what is the whole business of the trader's account, but to over-reach him who trusts to his memory? But were that not so, what can there great and noble be expected from him whose attention is forever fixed upon balancing his books, and watching over his expenses? And at best, let frugality and parsimony be the virtues of the merchant, how much is his punctual dealing below a gentleman's charity to the poor, or hospitality among his neighbors?

Captain Sentry observed Sir Andrew very diligent in hearing Sir Roger, and had a mind to turn the discourse, by taking notice in general, from the highest to the lowest parts of human society, there was a secret, though unjust, way among men, of indulging the seeds of ill nature and envy, by comparing their own state of life to that of another, and grudging the approach of their neighbor to their own happiness; and on the other side, he who is the less at his ease, repines at the other who, he thinks, has unjustly the advantage over him. Thus the civil and military lists look upon each other with much ill nature; the soldier repines at the courtier's power, and the courtier rallies the soldier's honor; or, to come to lower instances, the private men in the horse and foot of an army, the carmen and coachmen in the city streets, mutually look upon each other with ill will, when they are in competition for quarters or the way, in their respective motions.

"It is very well, good captain," interrupted Sir Andrew: "you may attempt to turn the discourse if you think fit; but I must however have a word or two with Sir Roger, who, I see, thinks he has paid me off, and been very severe upon the merchant. I shall not," continued he, "at this time remind Sir Roger of the great and noble monuments of charity and public spirit, which have been erected by merchants since the Reformation, but at present content myself with what he allows us, parsimony and

frugality.   If it were consistent with the quality of so ancient a
baronet as Sir Roger, to keep an account, or measure things by
the most infallible way, that of numbers, he would prefer our
parsimony to his hospitality.   If to drink so many hogsheads is
to be hospitable, we do not contend for the fame of that virtue;
but it would be worth while to consider, whether so many artificers at work ten days together by my appointment, or so many
peasants made merry on Sir Roger's charge, are the men more
obliged?   I believe the families of the artificers will thank me,
more than the households of the peasants shall Sir Roger.   Sir
Roger gives to his men, but I place mine above the necessity or
obligation of my bounty.   I am in very little pain for the Roman
proverb upon the Carthaginian traders; the Romans were their
professed enemies: I am only sorry no Carthaginian histories
have come to our hands; we might have been taught perhaps
by them some proverbs against the Roman generosity, in fighting
for and bestowing other people's goods.   But since Sir Roger
has taken occasion from an old proverb to be out of humor with
merchants, it should be no offense to offer one not quite so old
in their defense.   When a man happens to break in Holland, they
say of him that 'he has not kept true accounts.'   This phrase,
perhaps, among us, would appear a soft or humorous way of
speaking, but with that exact nation it bears the highest reproach;
for a man to be mistaken in the calculation of his expense, in
his ability to answer future demands, or to be impertinently san-
guine in putting his credit to too great adventure, are all instances of as much infamy as with gayer nations to be failing in
courage or common honesty.

"Numbers are so much the measure of everything that is
valuable, that it is not possible to demonstrate the success of any
action, or the prudence of any undertaking, without them.   I say
this in answer to what Sir Roger is pleased to say, 'that little
that is truly noble can be expected from one who is ever poring
on his cash-book, or balancing his accounts.'   When I have my
returns from abroad, I can tell to a shilling, by the help of num-

bers, the profit or loss by my adventure; but I ought also to be able to show that I had reason for making it, either from my own experience or that of other people, or from a reasonable presumption that my returns will be sufficient to answer my expense and hazard; and this is never to be done without the skill of numbers. For instance, if I am to trade to Turkey, I ought beforehand to know the demand of our manufactures there, as well as of their silks in England, and the customary prices that are given for both in each country. I ought to have a clear knowledge of these matters beforehand, that I may presume upon sufficient returns to answer the charge of the cargo I have fitted out, the freight and assurance out and home, the custom to the Queen, and the interest of my own money, and besides all these expenses a reasonable profit to myself. Now what is there of scandal in this skill? What has the merchant done, that he should be so little in the good graces of Sir Roger? He throws down no man's inclosures, and tramples upon no man's corn; he takes nothing from the industrious laborer; he pays the poor man for his work; he communicates his profit with mankind; by the preparation of his cargo and the manufacture of his returns, he furnishes employment and subsistence to greater numbers than the richest nobleman; and even the nobleman is obliged to him for finding out foreign markets for the produce of his estate, and for making a great addition to his rents; and yet 'tis certain, that none of all these things could be done by him without the exercise of his skill in numbers.

"This is the economy of the merchant; and the conduct of the gentleman must be the same, unless by scorning to be the steward, he resolves the steward shall be the gentleman. The gentleman, no more than the merchant, is able, without the help of numbers, to account for the success of any action, or the prudence of any adventure. If, for instance, the chase is his whole adventure, his only returns must be the stag's horns in the great hall, and the fox's nose upon the stable door. Without doubt Sir Roger knows the full value of these returns; and if beforehand he had computed the charges of the chase, a gentleman of his discretion would certainly have hanged up all his dogs, he would never have brought back so many fine horses to the kennel, he would never have gone so often, like a blast, over fields of corn. If such too had been the conduct of all his ancestors, he might truly have boasted at this day, that the antiquity of his family had never been sullied by a trade; a merchant had never been permitted with his whole estate to purchase a room for his picture in the gallery of the Coverleys, or to claim his descent from the maid of honor. But 'tis very happy for Sir Roger that the merchant paid so dear for his ambition. 'Tis the misfortune of many other gentlemen to turn out of the seats of their ancestors, to make way for such new masters as have been more exact in their accounts than themselves; and certainly he deserves the estate a great deal better, who has got it by his industry, than he who has lost it by his negligence." T.

SIR ROGER IN LONDON.

[*ADDISON, in SPECTATOR, No. 269. Tuesday, January 8, 1711-12.*]

> "*Ævo rarissima nostro
> Simplicitas.*" [1]
>
> OVID, Ars Amatoria, Lib. I. 241.

I WAS this morning surprised with a great knocking at the door, when my landlady's daughter came up to me, and told me, that there was a man below desired to speak with me. Upon my asking her who it was, she told me it was a very grave elderly person, but that she did not know his name. I immediately went down to him, and found him to be the coachman of my worthy friend Sir Roger de Coverley. He told me that his master came to town last night, and would be glad to take a turn

---

[1] Dryden's translation: "Most rare is now our old simplicity."

with me in Gray's Inn[1] walks. As I was wondering in myself what had brought Sir Roger to town, not having lately received any letter from him, he told me that his master was come up to get a sight of Prince Eugene,[2] and that he desired I would immediately meet him.

I was not a little pleased with the curiosity of the old knight, though I did not much wonder at it, having heard him say more than once in private discourse, that he looked upon Prince Eugenio (for so the knight always calls him) to be a greater man than Scanderbeg.[3]

I was no sooner come into Gray's Inn walks, but I heard my friend upon the terrace hemming twice or thrice to himself with great vigor, for he loves to clear his pipes in good air (to make use of his own phrase) and is not a little pleased with any one who takes notice of the strength which he still exerts in his morning hems.

I was touched with a secret joy at the sight of the good old man, who before he saw me was engaged in conversation with a beggar-man that had asked an alms of him. I could hear my friend chide him for not finding out some work; but at the same time saw him put his hand in his pocket and give him sixpence.

Our salutations were very hearty on both sides, consisting of many kind shakes of the hand, and several affectionate looks which we cast upon one another. After which the knight told me my good friend his chaplain was very well, and much at my service, and that the Sunday before he had made a most incomparable sermon out of Dr. Barrow. " I have left," says he, " all

[1] See Note 2, p. 20.

[2] Prince Eugene of Savoy (1663–1736) was a celebrated general, serving principally in Austria and in the wars of the Spanish Succession. He, with the Duke of Marlborough, commanded the allies in the battle of Blenheim. He afterwards drove the French out of Italy.

[3] Scanderbeg, i.e., Iskander (Alexander) Bey, the Turkish name and title of George Castriota (1404–67), was a celebrated Albanian prince. He renounced Mohammedanism, and was principally engaged at war with the Turks for Albanian independence.

my affairs in his hands, and being willing to lay an obligation upon him, have deposited with him thirty marks, to be distributed among his poor parishioners."

He then proceeded to acquaint me with the welfare of Will Wimble. Upon which he put his hand into his fob and presented me in his name with a tobacco-stopper, telling me that Will had been busy all the beginning of the winter in turning great quantities of them; and that he made a present of one to every gentleman in the country who has good principles, and smokes. He added, that poor Will was at present under great tribulation, for that Tom Touchy had taken the law of him for cutting some hazel sticks out of one of his hedges.

Among other pieces of news which the knight brought from his country seat, he informed me that Moll White was dead; and that about a month after her death the wind was so very high, that it blew down the end of one of his barns. "But for my own part," says Sir Roger, "I do not think that the old woman had any hand in it."

He afterwards fell into an account of the diversions which had passed in his house during the holidays; for Sir Roger, after the laudable custom of his ancestors, always keeps open house at Christmas. I learned from him that he had killed eight fat hogs for the season, that he had dealt about his chines very liberally amongst his neighbors, and that in particular he had sent a string of hog's-puddings[1] with a pack of cards[2] to every poor family in the parish. "I have often thought," says Sir Roger, "it happens very well that Christmas should fall out in the middle of the winter. It is the most dead uncomfortable time of the year, when the poor people would suffer very much from their poverty and cold, if they had not good cheer, warm fires, and Christmas gambols to support them. I love to rejoice their poor hearts at this season, and to see the whole village merry in my great hall. I

---

[1] Sausages.

[2] Playing cards was one of the chief amusements during the evenings at Christmas-tide in old England.

allow a double quantity of malt to my small-beer, and set it a-running for twelve days to every one that calls for it. I have always a piece of cold beef and a mince pie upon the table, and am wonderfully pleased to see my tenants pass away a whole evening in playing their innocent tricks, and smutting one another. Our friend Will Wimble is as merry as any of them, and shows a thousand roguish tricks upon these occasions."

I was very much delighted with the reflection of my old friend, which carried so much goodness in it. He then launched out into the praise of the late act of Parliament for securing the Church of England,[1] and told me, with great satisfaction, that he believed it already began to take effect, for that a rigid Dissenter, who chanced to dine at his house on Christmas Day, had been observed to eat very plentifully of his plum porridge.

After having dispatched all our country matters, Sir Roger made several inquiries concerning the Club, and particularly of his old antagonist Sir Andrew Freeport. He asked me with a kind of smile, whether Sir Andrew had not taken advantage of his absence, to vent among them some of his republican doctrines; but soon after gathering up his countenance into a more than ordinary seriousness, "Tell me truly," says he, "don't you think Sir Andrew had a hand in the Pope's procession"[2] — but without giving me time to answer him, "Well, well," says he, "I know you are a wary man, and do not care to talk of public matters."

The knight then asked me, if I had seen Prince Eugenio, and made me promise to get him a stand in some convenient place where he might have a full sight of that extraordinary man, whose presence does so much honor to the British nation. He dwelt very long on the praises of this great general, and I found

[1] This refers to one of the numerous laws made by England to protect her state Church, in this particular case against occasional conformity.

[2] The anniversary of the accession of Queen Elizabeth, Nov. 17, was for many years celebrated by the citizens of London by a procession, which was headed by an effigy of the Pope. After the parade the figure was burned.

that, since I was with him in the country, he had drawn many observations together out of his reading in Baker's " Chronicle,"[1] and other authors, who always lie in his hall window, which very much redound to the honor of this prince.

Having passed away the greatest part of the morning in hearing the knight's reflections, which were partly private, and partly political, he asked me if I would smoke a pipe with him over a dish of coffee at Squires's.[2] As I love the old man, I take delight in complying with everything that is agreeable to him, and accordingly waited on him to the coffee-house, where his venerable figure drew upon us the eyes of the whole room. He had no sooner seated himself at the upper end of the high table, but he called for a clean pipe, a paper of tobacco, a dish of coffee, a wax candle, and the Supplement[3] with such an air of cheerfulness and good humor, that all the boys in the coffee-room (who seemed to take pleasure in serving him) were at once employed on his several errands, insomuch that nobody else could come at a dish of tea, till the knight had got all his conveniences about him.

L.

---

[1] Baker's Chronicle of the Kings of England (1641). The author, Sir Richard Baker (1568–1645), was for many years confined in Fleet Prison, and there turned author. Of his Chronicle, he assures us, that, if all other chronicles were lost, this only would be sufficient to supply all necessary and accurate information.

[2] Squires's Coffee House (Fulwards Rents) was named for the owner, and was much patronized by the benchers and students of Gray's Inn.

[3] This reference is evidently to a paper published at that period.

SIR ROGER IN WESTMINSTER ABBEY.

[*ADDISON, in SPECTATOR, No. 329. Tuesday, March 18, 1711–12.*]

"Ire tamen restat, Numa quo devenit et ancus." [1]

HORACE, Lib. I. Ep. vi. 27.

MY friend Sir Roger de Coverley told me t'other night, that he had been reading my paper upon Westminster Abbey,[2] in which, says he, there are a great many ingenious fancies. He told me at the same time, that he observed I had promised another paper upon the tombs, and that he should be glad to go and see them with me, not having visited them since he had read history. I could not at first imagine how this came into the knight's head, till I recollected that he had been very busy all last summer upon Baker's "Chronicle," which he has quoted several times in his disputes with Sir Andrew Freeport since his last coming to town. Accordingly I promised to call upon him the next morning, that we might go together to the Abbey.

I found the knight under his butler's hands, who always shaves him. He was no sooner dressed, than he called for a glass of the Widow Trueby's water, which he told me he always drank before

---

[1] Free translation: —

"With Ancus, and with Numa, kings of Rome,
We must decend into the silent tomb."

[2] Westminster Abbey, the most celebrated religious edifice in England, stands on the bank of the Thames, in London. A church was built here by King Sebert in the seventh century, which was replaced with a stone edifice by Edward the Confessor in the middle of the eleventh century. Much of the existing building was put up by Henry III. in the thirteenth century; but important additions and alterations were made at intervals down to the time of Sir Christopher Wren (1700), who designed the two great western towers. The Abbey has been the place of coronation of the British sovereigns since the time of Harold (1066), and it contains the tombs of most of them, as well as of very many of England's greatest men, — soldiers, philosophers, poets, and scientists.

he went abroad. He recommended me to a dram of it at the same time, with so much heartiness, that I could not forbear drinking it. As soon as I had got it down, I found it very unpalatable; upon which the knight observing that I had made several wry faces, told me that he knew I should not like it at first, but that it was the best thing in the world against the stone or gravel.

I could have wished indeed that he had acquainted me with the virtues of it sooner; but it was too late to complain, and I knew what he had done was out of good will. Sir Roger told me further, that he looked upon it to be very good for a man whilst he staid in town, to keep off infection, and that he got together a quantity of it upon the first news of the sickness being at Dantzic:[1] when of a sudden turning short to one of his servants, who stood behind him, he bid him call a hackney-coach, and take care it was an elderly man that drove it.

He then resumed his discourse upon Mrs. Trueby's water, telling me that the Widow Trueby was one who did more good than all the doctors and apothecaries in the county: that she distilled every poppy that grew within five miles of her; that she distributed her water gratis among all sorts of people; to which the knight added, that she had a very great jointure, and that the whole country would fain have it a match between him and her; "and truly," says Sir Roger, "if I had not been engaged, perhaps I could not have done better."

His discourse was broken off by his man's telling him he had called a coach. Upon our going to it, after having cast his eye upon the wheels, he asked the coachman if his axle-tree was good; upon the fellow's telling him he would warrant it, the knight turned to me, told me he looked like an honest man, and went in without further ceremony.

We had not gone far, when Sir Roger popping out his head, called the coachman down from his box, and upon his present-

---

[1] A town of North Germany, built in 1165. This refers to a plague which visited it in 1709.

ing himself at the window, asked him if he smoked; as I was considering what this would end in, he bid him stop by the way at any good tobacconist's, and take in a roll of their best Virginia.[1] Nothing material happened in the remaining part of our journey, till we were set down at the west end of the Abbey.

As we went up the body of the church, the knight pointed at the trophies upon one of the new monuments, and cried out, "A brave man, I warrant him!" Passing afterwards by Sir Cloudsly Shovel,[2] he flung his hand that way, and cried "Sir Cloudsly Shovel! a very gallant man!" As we stood before Busby's tomb,[3] the knight uttered himself again after the same manner, "Dr. Busby, a great man! he whipped my grandfather; a very great man! I should have gone to him myself, if I had not been a blockhead; a very great man!"

We were immediately conducted into the little chapel on the right hand. Sir Roger planting himself at our historian's elbow, was very attentive to everything he said, particularly to the account he gave us of the lord who had cut off the King of Morocco's head. Among several other figures, he was very well pleased to see the statesman Cecil[4] upon his knees; and, concluding them all to be great men, was conducted to the figure which represents that martyr to good housewifery, who died by the prick of a needle. Upon our interpreter's telling us, that she was a maid of honor to Queen Elizabeth,[5] the knight was

[1] Tobacco.

[2] Sir Cloudsly Shovel (1650–1707) was a distinguished English admiral, knighted for his services at Bantry Bay, and prominent in the battle of La Hogue.

[3] Dr. Richard Busby (1606–95) was head master of Westminster School for fifty-eight years (1638–95). The recollection of his severity long invested his monument in Westminster Abbey with a peculiar awe.

[4] Robert Cecil, Earl of Salisbury (1560–1612), an able English statesman, was prime-minister under James I., and Lord Treasurer of England.

[5] Queen Elizabeth (1533–1603), the most famous of England's queens, reigned from 1558 to 1603. She was the daughter of Henry VIII. and Anne Boleyn.

very inquisitive into her name and family; and after having re-garded her finger for some time, "I wonder," says he, "that Sir Richard Baker has said nothing of her in his 'Chronicle.'"

We were then conveyed to the two coronation chairs, where my old friend, after having heard that the stone underneath the most ancient of them, which was brought from Scotland, was called Jacob's Pillar,[1] sat himself down in the chair; and looking like the figure of an old Gothic king, asked our interpreter, what authority they had to say, that Jacob had ever been in Scotland? The fellow, instead of returning him an answer, told him, that he hoped his honor would pay his forfeit. I could observe Sir Roger a little ruffled upon being thus trepanned; but our guide not insisting upon his demand, the knight soon recovered his good humor, and whispered in my ear, that if Will Wimble were with us, and saw those two chairs, it would go hard but he would get a tobacco-stopper out of one or t'other of them.

Sir Roger, in the next place, laid his hand upon Edward III.'s[2] sword, and leaning upon the pommel of it, gave us the whole history of the Black Prince; concluding, that in Sir Rich-ard Baker's opinion, Edward III. was one of the greatest princes that ever sat upon the English throne.

---

[1] Jacob's Pillar or stone, a fragment of sandstone rock inclosed in the cor-onation chair at Westminster. It is of the same geological formation as the rock of the west coast of Scotland, and probably came from that locality. It formed part of the coronation chair at Scone, Scotland, from the ninth cen-tury until Edward I. captured it and transferred it to Westminster. Its name is due to a myth connected with it as early as the fourteenth century, which held that this rock was part of the pillar on which Jacob or Abraham slept at Bethel; that it was transported to Egypt, and thence to Sicily or Spain, in Moses' time; that from Spain it was carried off by Simon Brech, the son of Milo, to Ireland, where, on the sacred hill of Tara, it became "Lia Fail," or the Stone of Destiny. Fergus, the founder of the Scottish mon-archy, is supposed to have removed it to Dunstaffnage, Scotland, whence Kenneth II. removed it to Scone, A.D. 840.

[2] Edward III. (1312–77), the son of Edward II., was proclaimed king in 1327. He won the battle of Crècy in 1347. He was the father of the Black Prince, the hero of the battle of Poitiers.

We were then shown Edward the Confessor's [1] tomb; upon which Sir Roger acquainted us, that he was the first who touched for the evil; [2] and afterwards Henry IV.'s, [3] upon which he shook his head, and told us there was fine reading in the casualties in that reign.

Our conductor then pointed to that monument where there is the figure of one of our English kings without a head; and upon giving us to know, that the head, which was of beaten silver, had been stolen away several years since: "Some Whig, I'll warrant you," says Sir Roger; "you ought to lock up your kings better; they will carry off the body too, if you don't take care."

The glorious names of Henry V. [4] and Queen Elizabeth gave the knight great opportunities of shining, and of doing justice to Sir Richard Baker, who, as our knight observed with some surprise, had a great many kings in him, whose monuments he had not seen in the Abbey.

For my own part, I could not but be pleased to see the knight show such an honest passion for the glory of his country, and such a respectful gratitude to the memory of its princes.

I must not omit, that the benevolence of my good old friend, which flows out towards every one he converses with, made him very kind to our interpreter, whom he looked upon as an extraordinary man; for which reason he shook him by the hand at

[1] Edward the Confessor (1004–66), son of Ethelred, became King of the Anglo-Saxons in 1042.

[2] Scrofula was formerly called " King's Evil," because it was supposed that the disease could be cured by the touch of a truly anointed king.

[3] Henry IV. of England (1366–1413) was the son of John of Gaunt. He usurped the throne in 1399. He imprisoned his predecessor, Richard II., and is supposed to have ordered his murder. He kept the legitimate heir, young Edward Mortimer, in custody for fourteen years. He passed a statute for burning heretics, and was constantly brawling with his nobles, his neighbors in Scotland, France, and with his son, afterwards Henry V.

[4] Henry V. of England (1388–1422), oldest son of Henry IV., distinguished himself at the battle of Shrewsbury, and defeated the French at Agincourt. He married Catherine, daughter of Charles VI.

parting, telling him, that he should be very glad to see him at his lodgings in Norfolk Buildings, and talk over these matters with him more at leisure.   L.

SIR ROGER AND BEARDS.

[*Budgell, in Spectator, No. 331.   Thursday, March 20, 1711-12.*]

"Stolidam præbet tibi vellere barbam." [1]
PERSIUS, Sat. ii. 28.

WHEN I was last with my friend Sir Roger in Westminster Abbey, I observed that he stood longer than ordinary before the bust of a venerable old man.   I was at a loss to guess the reason of it, when after some time he pointed to the figure, and asked me if I did not think that our forefathers looked much wiser in their beards than we do without them?   "For my part," says he, "when I am walking in my gallery in the country, and see my ancestors, who many of them died before they were of my age, I cannot forbear regarding them as so many old patriarchs, and at the same time looking upon myself as an idle smock-faced young fellow.   I love to see your Abrahams, your Isaacs, and your Jacobs, as we have them in old pieces of tapestry, with beards below their girdles, that cover half the hangings."   The knight added, if I would recommend beards in one of my papers, and endeavor to restore human faces to their ancient dignity, that upon a month's warning he would undertake to lead up the fashion himself in a pair of whiskers.

I smiled at my friend's fancy; but after we parted, could not forbear reflecting on the metamorphoses our faces have undergone in this particular.

The beard, conformable to the notion of my friend Sir Roger, was for many ages looked upon as the type of wisdom.   Lucian [2]

---

1 "Holds out his foolish beard for thee to pluck."
2 Lucian (born about A.D. 120) was one of the wittiest and most origi-

more than once rallies the philosophers of his time, who endeavored to rival one another in beard; and represents a learned man who stood for a professorship in philosophy, as unqualified for it by the shortness of his beard.

Ælian,[1] in his account of Zoilus,[2] the pretended critic, who wrote against Homer[3] and Plato,[4] and thought himself wiser than all who had gone before him, tells us that this Zoilus had a very long beard that hung down upon his breast, but no hair upon his head, which he always kept close shaved, regarding, it seems, the hairs of his head as so many suckers, which if they had been suffered to grow, might have drawn away the nourishment from his chin, and by that means have starved his beard.

I have read somewhere that one of the popes refused to accept an edition of a saint's works, which were presented to him, because the saint in his effigies before the book, was drawn without a beard.

We see by these instances what homage the world has formerly paid to beards; and that a barber was not then allowed to make those depredations on the faces of the learned, which have been permitted him of later years.

Accordingly several wise nations have been so extremely jealous of the least ruffle offered to their beard, that they seem to have fixed the point of honor principally in that part. The

nal of Greek writers. He lived at Athens. His principal works are the Dialogues.

[1] Ælian, a native of Præneste, Italy, lived in the early part of the third century. Although an Italian by birth, he wrote Greek. His works are scrappy and gossiping, and cover a great variety of subjects,— historical, biographical, antiquarian, narratives, and anecdotes.

[2] A Greek critic and grammarian (of uncertain date), noted chiefly for his criticism of Homer.

[3] Homer (born about 1000 B.C.), author of The Iliad and The Odyssey, was the greatest poet of antiquity and the most celebrated writer that ever lived.

[4] Plato (born about 430 B.C.), a pupil of Socrates, was one of the most illustrious Greek philosophers of all time. He wrote the famous Dialogues.

Spaniards were wonderfully tender in this particular.   Don Quevedo,[1] in his third "Vision on the Last Judgment," has carried
the humor very far, when he tells us that one of his vainglorious
countrymen, after having received sentence, was taken into custody by a couple of evil spirits; but that his guides happening to
disorder his mustaches, they were forced to recompose them with
a pair of curling-irons before they could get him to file off.

If we look into the history of our own nation, we shall find
that the beard flourished in the Saxon Heptarchy, but was very
much discouraged under the Norman line.   It shot out, however,
from time to time, in several reigns under different shapes.   The
last effort it made seems to have been in Queen Mary's[2] days, as
the curious reader may find, if he pleases to peruse the figures
of Cardinal Pole,[3] and Bishop Gardiner;[4] though at the same
time, I think it may be questioned, if zeal against popery has
not induced our Protestant painters to extend the beards of these
two persecutors beyond their natural dimensions, in order to
make them appear the more terrible.

I find but few beards worth taking notice of in the reign of
King James I.[5]

---

[1] Francisco Gomez Quevedo (1580–1645) was a Spanish author and
satirist.   He wrote both prose and verse.   His best-known book is Visions.

[2] Queen Mary, or "Bloody Mary," (1516–58), reigned in England from
1553 to 1558.   She was the daughter of Henry VIII. and Catharine of
Aragon.

[3] Cardinal Reginald Pole (1500–55) was a celebrated English cardinal and
scholar.   He lost favor with Henry VIII. by opposing the divorce of Catharine of Aragon.   He was restored to power by Queen Mary, and succeeded
Cranmer as Archbishop of Canterbury.

[4] Bishop Stephen Gardiner (1483–1555) was an English prelate and statesman.   A friend to Henry VIII., he became Bishop of Winchester.   Under
Queen Mary he became chancellor of England, and the chief foe of Protest-
antism.

[5] James I. (1566–1625) of England was James VI. of Scotland, son of
Mary Queen of Scots and Lord Darnley.   He became King of England upon
the death of Elizabeth.   He came to the Scottish throne when only a year
old, and thus reigned fifty-eight years, twenty-two of them in England.

During the civil wars there appeared one, which makes too great a figure in story to be passed over in silence; I mean that of the redoubted Hudibras,[1] an account of which Butler has transmitted to posterity in the following lines:—

> " His tawny beard was th' equal grace
> Both of his wisdom, and his face;
> In cut and dye so like a tile,
> A sudden view it would beguile:
> The upper part thereof was whey,
> The nether orange mixt with gray."

The whisker continued for some time among us after the expiration of beards; but this is a subject which I shall not here enter upon, having discussed it at large in a distinct treatise, which I keep by me in manuscript, upon the mustache.

If my friend Sir Roger's project, of introducing beards, should take effect, I fear the luxury of the present age would make it a very expensive fashion. There is no question but the beaus would soon provide themselves with false ones of the lightest colors, and the most immoderate lengths. A fair beard, of the tapestry size Sir Roger seems to approve, could not come under twenty guineas. The famous golden beard of Æsculapius[2] would hardly be more valuable than one made in the extravagance of the fashion.

Besides, we are not certain that the ladies would not come into the mode, when they take the air on horseback. They already appear in hats and feathers, coats and periwigs; and I see no

---

[1] The title of a famous satire on the Puritans, by Samuel Butler (1612–80), published in London in three parts, 1663, 1664, 1678. Many well-known people were satirized. The hero, Hudibras, a Presbyterian, supposed to characterize Sir Samuel Lecke or Sir Henry Roswell, sets out on an expedition against the follies and amusements of his time.

[2] In Greek mythology, the god of medicine, supposed to be the son of Apollo and Coronis. According to story he was annihilated by Jupiter with a bolt of lightning because he had restored a number of persons to life. Æsculapius was worshiped very generally throughout all Greece, the principal seat of his shrine being Epidaurus. Serpents were connected with his worship.

reason why we [may] not suppose that they would have their riding-beards on the same occasion.

I may give the moral of this discourse in another paper.

X.

SIR ROGER AT THE PLAY.

[*ADDISON, in* SPECTATOR, *No. 335.   Tuesday, March 25, 1712.*]

"*Respicere exemplar vitæ morumque jubebo
    Doctum imitatorem, et veras hinc ducere voces.*" [1]
                                        HORACE, Ars Poetica, v. 327.

M Y friend Sir Roger de Coverley, when we last met together at the Club, told me, that he had a great mind to see the new tragedy [2] with me, assuring me at the same time, that he had not been at a play these twenty years.   "The last I saw," said Sir Roger, "was 'The Committee,' [3] which I should not have gone to neither, had not I been told beforehand that it was a good Church-of-England comedy."   He then proceeded to inquire of me who this distressed mother was; and upon hearing that she was Hector's [4] widow, he told me that her husband was a brave man, and that when he was a schoolboy he had read his life at the end of the dictionary.   My friend asked me, in the next place, if there would not be some danger in coming home

---

[1] Francis's translation : —

                "Keep nature's great original in view,
                    And thence the living images pursue."

[2] The Distressed Mother, by Ambrose Philips (1671–1749), a play founded on the Andromaque of Racine.

[3] A comedy ridiculing the puritanical party, by Sir Robert Howard, published in 1665.

[4] The Trojan hero, oldest son of Priam and Hecuba, and the husband of Andromache.   He was the most valiant defender of Troy.   Killed by Achilles.

late, in case the Mohocks[1] should be abroad. "I assure you," says he, "I thought I had fallen into their hands last night; for I observed two or three lusty black men that followed me half-way up Fleet Street,[2] and mended their pace behind me, in proportion as I put on to get away from them. You must know," continued the knight with a smile, "I fancied they had a mind to hunt me; for I remember an honest gentleman in my neighborhood, who was served such a trick in King Charles II.'s[3] time; for which reason he has not ventured himself in town ever since. I might have shown them very good sport, had this been their design; for as I am an old fox-hunter, I should have turned and dodged, and have played them a thousand tricks they had never seen in their lives before." Sir Roger added, that "if these gentlemen had any such intention, they did not succeed very well in it: for I threw them out," says he, "at the end of Norfolk Street, where I doubled the corner, and got shelter in my lodgings before they could imagine what was become of me. However," says the knight, "if Captain Sentry will make one with us to-morrow night, and if you will both of you call upon me about four o'clock, that we may be at the house before it is full, I will have my own coach in readiness to attend you, for John tells me he has got the fore-wheels mended."

The captain, who did not fail to meet me there at the appointed hour, bid Sir Roger fear nothing, for that he had put on the same sword which he made use of at the battle of Steenkirk.[4] Sir Roger's servants, and among the rest my old friend the but-

---

[1] The slang name of a gang of London ruffians. The name is probably corrupted from that of the Mohawk Indians.

[2] One of the most familiar thoroughfares in London. It runs from Ludgate Hill to the Strand. It derived its name from a stream, the Fleet. In 1228 it was called Fleet Bridge Street.

[3] Charles II. (1630–85) was the oldest son of Charles I. He was defeated at the battle of Worcester (1651) by Cromwell. He escaped to France, where he remained during Cromwell's ascendency. He was restored to the English throne May, 1660.

[4] Battle of Steenkirk, or Enghien, a town in southwestern Belgium. Here

ler, had, I found, provided themselves with good oaken plants, to attend their master upon this occasion. When he had placed him in his coach, with myself at his left hand, the captain before him, and his butler at the head of his footmen in the rear, we convoyed him in safety to the playhouse, where, after having marched up the entry in good order, the captain and I went in with him, and seated him betwixt us in the pit. As soon as the house was full, and the candles lighted, my old friend stood up and looked about him with that pleasure, which a mind seasoned with humanity naturally feels in itself, at the sight of a multitude of people who seem pleased with one another, and partake of the same common entertainment. I could not but fancy to myself, as the old man stood up in the middle of the pit, that he made a very proper center to a tragic audience. Upon the entering of Pyrrhus,[1] the knight told me, that he did not believe the King of France himself had a better strut. I was indeed very attentive to my old friend's remarks, because I looked upon them as a piece of natural criticism, and was well pleased to hear him at the conclusion of almost every scene, telling me that he could not imagine how the play would end. One while he appeared much concerned for Andromache;[2] and a little while after as much for Hermione:[3] and was extremely puzzled to think what would become of Pyrrhus.

When Sir Roger saw Andromache's obstinate refusal to her lover's importunities, he whispered me in the ear, that he was sure she would never have him; to which he added, with a more than ordinary vehemence, "You can't imagine, sir, what 'tis to have

the British under William III. were defeated by the French under Marshal Luxemburg, July, 1692.

[1] Pyrrhus, also called Neoptolemus, was a fabulous Greek warrior, son of Achilles, one of the heroes concealed in the Wooden Horse at the capture of Troy.

[2] A Trojan woman, wife of Hector, noted for her beauty and virtue. She became the captive of Pyrrhus at the fall of Troy.

[3] Daughter of Menelaus and Helen. She married Pyrrhus, and after his death became the wife of Orestes.

to do with a widow.' Upon Pyrrhus's threatening afterwards
to leave her, the knight shook his head, and muttered to himself,
" Ay, do if you can." This part dwelt so much upon my friend's
imagination, that at the close of the third act, as I was thinking
of something else, he whispered in my ear, " These widows, sir,
are the most perverse creatures in the world. But pray," says
he, " you that are a critic, is this play according to your dramatic
rules, as you call them? Should your people in tragedy always
talk to be understood? Why, there is not a single sentence in
this play that I do not know the meaning of."

The fourth act very luckily began before I had time to give
the old gentleman an answer: " Well," says the knight, sitting
down with great satisfaction, " I suppose we are now to see
Hector's ghost." He then renewed his attention, and, from time
to time, fell a-praising the widow. He made, indeed, a little mistake as to one of her pages, whom at his first entering, he took
for Astyanax;[1] but he quickly set himself right in that particular,
though, at the same time, he owned he should have been very
glad to have seen the little boy, who, says he, must needs be a
very fine child by the account that is given of him. Upon Hermione's going off with a menace to Pyrrhus, the audience gave a
loud clap; to which Sir Roger added, " On my word, a notable
young baggage!"

As there was a very remarkable silence and stillness in the
audience during the whole action, it was natural for them to take
the opportunity of these intervals between the acts, to express
their opinion of the players, and of their respective parts. Sir
Roger hearing a cluster of them praise Orestes,[2] struck in with
them, and told them, that he thought his friend Pylades[3] was a

[1] Astyanax, also called Scamander, was the son of Hector and Andromache. Killed in infancy at siege of Troy.

[2] Orestes, son of Agamemnon and Clytemnestra, became King of
Mycenæ.

[3] Pylades was the son of Strophimus, King of Phoces, and cousin and
friend of Orestes.

very sensible man; as they were afterwards applauding Pyrrhus, Sir Roger put in a second time; "And let me tell you," says he, "though he speaks but little, I like the old fellow in whiskers as well as any of them." Captain Sentry seeing two or three wags who sat near us, lean with an attentive ear towards Sir Roger, and fearing lest they should smoke [1] the knight, plucked him by the elbow, and whispered something in his ear, that lasted till the opening of the fifth act. The knight was wonderfully attentive to the account which Orestes gives of Pyrrhus's death, and at the conclusion of it, told me it was such a bloody piece of work, that he was glad it was not done upon the stage. Seeing afterwards Orestes in his raving fit, he grew more than ordinary serious, and took occasion to moralize (in his way) upon an evil conscience, adding, that Orestes, in his madness, looked as if he saw something.

As we were the first that came into the house, so we were the last that went out of it; being resolved to have a clear passage for our old friend, whom we did not care to venture among the jostling of the crowd. Sir Roger went out fully satisfied with his entertainment, and we guarded him to his lodgings in the same manner that we brought him to the playhouse; being highly pleased, for my own part, not only with the performance of the excellent piece which had been presented, but with the satisfaction which it had given to the good old man. L.

---

[1] To quiz or ridicule.

WILL HONEYCOMB AT THE CLUB.

[*BUDGELL, in SPECTATOR, No. 359. Tuesday, April 22, 1712.*]

"Torva leæna lupum sequitur, lupus ipse capellam;
Florentem cytisum sequitur lasciva capella." [1]

VIRGIL, Eclogues, vi. 63.

AS we were at the Club last night, I observed that my friend Sir Roger, contrary to his usual custom, sat very silent, and instead of minding what was said by the company, was whistling to himself in a very thoughtful mood, and playing with a cork. I jogged Sir Andrew Freeport who sat between us; and as we were both observing him, we saw the knight shake his head, and heard him say to himself, "A foolish woman! I can't believe it." Sir Andrew gave him a gentle pat upon the shoulder, and offered to lay him a bottle of wine that he was thinking of the widow. My old friend started, and recovering out of his brown study, told Sir Andrew that once in his life he had been in the right. In short, after some little hesitation, Sir Roger told us in the fullness of his heart that he had just received a letter from his steward, which acquainted him that his old rival and antagonist in the county, Sir David Dundrum, had been making a visit to the widow. "However," says Sir Roger, "I can never think that she'll have a man that's half a year older than I am, and a noted Republican into the bargain."

Will Honeycomb, who looks upon love as his particular province, interrupting our friend with a jaunty laugh; "I thought, knight," says he, "thou hadst lived long enough in the world, not to pin thy happiness upon one that is a woman and a widow. I think that without vanity I may pretend to know as much of the

---

[1] Warton's translation : —

" Lions the wolves, and wolves the kids pursue,
The kids sweet thyme,— and still I follow you."

female world as any man in Great Britain, though the chief of
my knowledge consists in this, that they are not to be known."
Will immediately, with his usual fluency, rambled into an account
of his own amours. "I am now," says he, "upon the verge of
fifty" (though by the way we all knew he was turned of threescore). "You may easily guess," continued Will, "that I have
not lived so long in the world without having had some thoughts
of settling in it, as the phrase is. To tell you truly, I have several times tried my fortune that way, though I can't much boast
of my success.

"I made my first addresses to a young lady in the country;
but when I thought things were pretty well drawing to a conclusion, her father happening to hear that I had formerly boarded
with a surgeon, the old put[1] forbid me his house, and within
a fortnight after married his daughter to a fox-hunter in the
neighborhood.

"I made my next applications to a widow, and attacked her
so briskly, that I thought myself within a fortnight of her. As I
waited upon her one morning, she told me that she intended to
keep her ready-money and jointure in her own hand, and desired
me to call upon her attorney in Lyon's Inn,[2] who would adjust
with me what it was proper for me to add to it. I was so re-
buffed by this overture, that I never inquired either for her or
her attorney afterwards.

"A few months after I addressed myself to a young lady, who
was an only daughter, and of a good family. I danced with her
at several balls, squeezed her by the hand, said soft things to her,
and, in short, made no doubt of her heart; and though my fortune was not equal to hers, I was in hopes that her fond father
would not deny her the man she had fixed her affections upon.
But as I went one day to the house in order to break the matter
to him, I found the whole family in confusion, and heard to my

---

[1] Pŭt, i.e., a rustic; an uncouth, awkward person.
[2] On Newcastle Street, Strand, London, an inn of chancery belonging to
the Inner Temple.

unspeakable surprise, that Miss Jenny was that very morning run away with the butler.

"I then courted a second widow, and am at a loss to this day how I came to miss her, for she had often commended my person and behavior. Her maid indeed told me one day, that her mistress had said she never saw a gentleman with such a spindle pair of legs as Mr. Honeycomb.

"After this I laid siege to four heiresses successively, and being a handsome young dog in those days, quickly made a breach in their hearts; but I don't know how it came to pass, though I seldom failed of getting the daughter's consent, I could never in my life get the old people on my side.

"I could give you an account of a thousand other unsuccessful attempts, particularly of one which I made some years since upon an old woman, whom I had certainly borne away with flying colors, if her relations had not come pouring in to her assistance from all parts of England; nay, I believe I should have got her at last, had not she been carried off by a hard frost."

As Will's transitions are extremely quick, he turned from Sir Roger, and applying himself to me, told me there was a passage in the book I had considered last Saturday, which deserved to be writ in letters of gold; and taking out a pocket Milton [1] read the following lines, which are part of one of Adam's speeches to Eve after the Fall.

> "Oh! why did our
> Creator wise! that peopled highest heav'n
> With spirits masculine, create at last
> This novelty on earth, this fair defect
> Of nature? and not fill the world at once
> With men, as angels, without feminine?
> Or find some other way to generate
> Mankind? This mischief had not then befall'n,
> And more that shall befall; innumerable
> Disturbances on earth through female snares,

---

[1] John Milton (1608–74), the immortal poet, excepting Shakespeare the most illustrious name in English literature, and author of Paradise Lost.

> And strait conjunction with this sex : for either
> He never shall find out fit mate, but such
> As some misfortune brings him, or mistake ;
> Or, whom he wishes most, shall seldom gain
> Through her perverseness ; but shall see her gain'd
> By a far worse ; or if she love, withheld
> By parents ; or his happiest choice too late
> Shall meet already link'd, and wedlock bound
> To a fell adversary, his hate or shame ;
> Which infinite calamity shall cause
> To human life, and household peace confound."

Sir Roger listened to this passage with great attention, and
desiring Mr. Honeycomb to fold down a leaf at the place, and
lend him his book, the knight put it up in his pocket, and told us
that he would read over those verses again before he went to
bed.   X.

SIR ROGER AT SPRING GARDEN.

[*ADDISON, in SPECTATOR, No. 383.   Tuesday, May 20, 1712.*]

"Criminibus debent hortos." [1]
JUVENAL, Sat. i. 75.

AS I was sitting in my chamber, and thinking on a subject
for my next "Spectator," I heard two or three irregular
bounces at my landlady's door, and upon the opening of it, a
loud cheerful voice inquiring whether the philosopher was at
home.   The child who went to the door answered very inno-
cently, that he did not lodge there.   I immediately recollected
that it was my good friend Sir Roger's voice ; and that I had
promised to go with him on the water to Spring Garden,[2] in case

---

[1] "A beauteous garden, but by vice maintain'd."

[2] Spring Garden, on the Surrey side of the Thames, was a short distance
east of Vauxhall Bridge, near Milbank.   It was opened in the reign of
Charles II., 1661.   It had extensive walks, numerous lamps, musical per-

it proved a good evening. The knight put me in mind of my promise from the bottom of the staircase, but told me that if I was speculating he would stay below till I had done. Upon my coming down, I found all the children of the family got about my old friend, and my landlady herself, who is a notable prating gossip, engaged in a conference with him; being mightily pleased with his stroking her little boy upon the head, and bidding him be a good child and mind his book.

We were no sooner come to the Temple Stairs,[1] but we were surrounded with a crowd of watermen, offering us their respective services. Sir Roger, after having looked about him very attentively, spied one with a wooden leg, and immediately gave him orders to get his boat ready. As we were walking towards it, "You must know," says Sir Roger, "I never make use of anybody to row me, that has not either lost a leg or an arm. I would rather bate him a few strokes of his oar, than not employ an honest man that has been wounded in the Queen's service. If I was a lord or a bishop, and kept a barge, I would not put a fellow in my livery that had not a wooden leg."

My old friend, after having seated himself, and trimmed the boat with his coachman, who, being a very sober man, always serves for ballast on these occasions, we made the best of our way for Vauxhall. Sir Roger obliged the waterman to give us the history of his right leg, and hearing that he had left it at La Hogue,[2] with many particulars which passed in that glorious action, the knight in the triumph of his heart made several reflections on the greatness of the British nation; as, that one Englishman could beat three Frenchmen; that we could never be in

formances, fireworks, etc. It was reöpened in 1732, and finally closed in 1859. Since 1785 it has been called Vauxhall Garden.

[1] Temple Stairs, or Temple Bridge, was a landing-place extending across two stone arches well into the Thames. It was built in 1621.

[2] A cape in Northwest France. On May 19, 1692, the English and Dutch fleets under Admirals Russell and Rook defeated the French under Admiral Tourville.

danger of popery so long as we took care of our fleet; that the Thames was the noblest river in Europe; that London Bridge[1] was a greater piece of work, than any of the seven wonders of the world; with many other honest prejudices which naturally cleave to the heart of a true Englishman.

After some short pause, the old knight turning about his head twice or thrice, to take a survey of this great metropolis, bid me observe how thick the city was set with churches, and that there was scarce a single steeple on this side Temple Bar.[2] "A most heathenish sight!" says Sir Roger: "there is no religion at this end of the town. The fifty new churches will very much mend the prospect; but church work is slow, church work is slow!"

I do not remember I have anywhere mentioned, in Sir Roger's character, his custom of saluting everybody that passes by him with a good-morrow or a good-night. This the old man does out of the overflowings of his humanity, though at the same time it renders him so popular among all his country neighbors, that it is thought to have gone a good way in making him once or twice knight of the shire. He cannot forbear this exercise of benevolence even in town, when he meets with any one in his morning or evening walk. It broke from him to several boats that passed by us upon the water; but to the knight's great surprise, as he gave the good-night to two or three young fellows a little before our landing, one of them, instead of returning the civility, asked us what queer old put we had in the boat, with a great deal of the like Thames ribaldry. Sir Roger seemed a little shocked at first, but at length assuming a face of magistracy,

---

[1] A stone bridge across the Thames from London to Southwark. It was built between 1176 and 1209, and consisted of 20 arches, a drawbridge, a chapel, etc. It was here the heads of traitors, and other offenders against the state, were exposed. Under Charles II. this custom was abolished.

[2] A gateway of Portland stone, which separated the Strand from Fleet Street. First mentioned in 1301. It was named from a chain or bar put up by the Knights Templars to mark the territory under the control of the city. The gateway is now destroyed, and a memorial now stands there which was unveiled Sept. 8, 1880.

told us, that if he were a Middesex[1] justice, he would make such vagrants know that her Majesty's subjects were no more to be abused by water than by land.

We were now arrived at Spring Garden, which is exquisitely pleasant at this time of year. When I considered the fragrancy of the walks and bowers, with the choirs of birds that sung upon the trees, and the loose tribe of people that walked under their shades, I could not but look upon the place as a kind of Mahometan Paradise. Sir Roger told me it put him in mind of a little coppice by his house in the country, which his chaplain used to call an aviary of nightingales. "You must understand," says the knight, "there is nothing in the world that pleases a man in love so much as your nightingale. Ah, Mr. Spectator! the many moonlight nights that I have walked by myself, and thought on the widow by the music of the nightingales!" He here fetched a deep sigh, and was falling into a fit of musing, when a mask, who came behind him, gave him a gentle tap upon the shoulder, and asked him if he would drink a bottle of mead with her? But the knight, being startled at so unexpected a familiarity, and displeased to be interrupted in his thoughts of the widow, told her, she was a wanton baggage, and bid her go about her business.

We concluded our walk with a glass of Burton ale, and a slice of hung beef. When we had done eating ourselves, the knight called a waiter to him, and bid him carry the remainder to the waterman that had but one leg. I perceived the fellow stared upon him at the oddness of the message, and was going to be saucy; upon which I ratified the knight's commands with a peremptory look.   I.

[1] The metropolitan county of England. Its name is a corruption of "Middlesexe" or "Middlesaxon."

SIR ROGER'S DEATH.

[*ADDISON, in SPECTATOR, No. 517.　Thursday, October 23, 1712.*]

"Heu pietas ! heu prisca fides." [1]
VIRGIL, Æneid, Lib. VI. 878.

WE last night received a piece of ill news at our Club, which very sensibly afflicted every one of us. I question not but my readers themselves will be troubled at the hearing of it. To keep them no longer in suspense, Sir Roger de Coverley is dead. He departed this life at his house in the country, after a few weeks' sickness. Sir Andrew Freeport has a letter from one of his correspondents in those parts, that informs him the old man caught a cold at the county-sessions, as he was very warmly promoting an address of his own penning, in which he succeeded according to his wishes. But this particular comes from a Whig justice of peace, who was always Sir Roger's enemy and antagonist. I have letters both from the chaplain and Captain Sentry which mention nothing of it, but are filled with many particulars to the honor of the good old man. I have likewise a letter from the butler, who took so much care of me last summer when I was at the knight's house. As my friend the butler mentions, in the simplicity of his heart, several circumstances the others have passed over in silence, I shall give my reader a copy of his letter, without any alteration or diminution.

HONORED SIR, — Knowing that you was my old master's good friend, I could not forbear sending you the melancholy news of his death, which has afflicted the whole country, as well as his poor servants, who loved him, I may say, better than we did our lives. I am afraid he caught his death the last county-sessions, where he would go to see justice done to a poor widow

---

[1] Dryden's translation : —

" Mirror of ancient faith !
Undaunted worth !　Inviolable truth ! "

woman, and her fatherless children, that had been wronged by a neighboring gentleman; for you know, sir, my good master was always the poor man's friend. Upon his coming home, the first complaint he made was, that he had lost his roast-beef stomach, not being able to touch a sirloin, which was served up according to custom; and you know he used to take great delight in it. From that time forward he grew worse and worse, but still kept a good heart to the last. Indeed we were once in great hope of his recovery, upon a kind message that was sent him from the widow lady whom he had made love to the forty last years of his life; but this only proved a light'ning before death. He has bequeathed to this lady, as a token of his love, a great pearl necklace, and a couple of silver bracelets set with jewels, which belonged to my good old lady his mother: he has bequeathed the fine white gelding, that he used to ride a hunting upon, to his chaplain, because he thought he would be kind to him, and has left you all his books. He has, moreover, bequeathed to the chaplain a very pretty tenement with good lands about it. It being a very cold day when he made his will, he left for mourning, to every man in the parish, a great frieze-coat, and to every woman a black riding-hood. It was a most moving sight to see him take leave of his poor servants, commending us all for our fidelity, whilst we were not able to speak a word for weeping. As we most of us are grown gray-headed in our dear master's service, he has left us pensions and legacies, which we may live very comfortably upon, the remaining part of our days. He has bequeathed a great deal more in charity, which is not yet come to my knowledge, and it is peremptorily said in the parish, that he has left money to build a steeple to the church; for he was heard to say some time ago, that if he lived two years longer, Coverley Church should have a steeple to it. The chaplain tells everybody that he made a very good end, and never speaks of him without tears. He was buried according to his own directions, among the family of the Coverleys, on the left hand of his father Sir Arthur. The coffin was carried by six of his tenants, and the pall held up by six of the quorum: the whole parish followed the corpse with heavy hearts, and in their mourning suits, the men in frieze, and the women in riding-hoods. Captain Sentry, my master's nephew, has taken possession of the Hall House, and the whole estate. When my old master saw him a little before his death, he shook him by the hand, and wished him joy of the estate which was falling to him, desiring him only to make good use of it, and to pay the several legacies, and the gifts of charity which he told him he had left as quit-rents upon the estate. The captain truly seems a courteous man, though he says but little. He makes much of those whom my master loved, and shows great kindness to the old house-dog, that you know my poor master was so fond of. It would have gone to your heart to have heard the moans the dumb creature made on the day of my master's death. He has ne'er joyed himself since;

no more has any of us. 'Twas the melancholiest day for the poor people that ever happened in Worcestershire.   This being all from, honored sir,

Your most sorrowful servant,

EDWARD BISCUIT.

P. S. — My master desired, some weeks before he died, that a book which comes up to you by the carrier should be given to Sir Andrew Freeport, in his name.

This letter, notwithstanding the poor butler's manner of writing it, gave us such an idea of our good old friend, that upon the reading of it there was not a dry eye in the Club. Sir Andrew opening the book, found it to be a collection of Acts of Parliament. There was in particular the Act of Uniformity, with some passages in it marked by Sir Roger's own hand.   Sir Andrew found that they related to two or three points, which he had disputed with Sir Roger the last time he appeared at the Club.   Sir Andrew, who would have been merry at such an incident on another occasion, at the sight of the old man's handwriting burst into tears, and put the book into his pocket.   Captain Sentry informs me, that the knight has left rings and mourning for every one in the Club.   O.

THE SPECTATOR

AN ORIGINAL NUMBER.—The notes in fine print appearing directly beneath the titles of the various papers in this volume, should prevent our losing sight of two important facts. The date reminds us that we are seeing a picture of English social life of two centuries ago. The phrase, "in Spectator No. —," recalls the fact that the essays are in reality selections from a "daily" paper whose 635 issues have found a permanent place in literature. It is natural that we should desire to turn from the present book or even from the octavo volumes of the early collected editions, to look at an original number. One of these first copies may sometimes be seen in a public library or in a private collection of manuscripts and rare books.

The *Spectator* was published in a part of London known as Little Britain, which was, two hundred years ago, the center of the bookselling and printing trade. Each number sold for a penny. It is reckoned that the circulation in a short time grew to eight or ten thousand. The papers were single folio sheets measuring twelve and one-half by eight inches and were printed on both sides in double column. THE SPECTATOR appeared in half inch letters at the top of the page. Below this were spaces inclosed by three parallel lines extending the full width of the sheet. In the first space was printed the Latin motto, which the Spectator says (in No. 221) was a word to the wise; in the second, the day and date of the issue. The special interest of an original number of the *Spectator* is found in the letterpress. This reveals the custom of the time in reference to such matters as capitalization, spelling, punctuation, and the use of italics. Every noun is capitalized. The spelling presents many surprises and indicates how much the orthography of our language has changed since 1711. On the other hand, we cannot discover much warrant for the fear expressed by writers of that day that the changes going on in the language might hinder people of later times from reading or appreciating early eighteenth century literature. A very free use of the comma and the semicolon is recognized; words are italicized more generally than now, and with less reason for it.

The ubiquitous advertisement of the modern press had made its appearance in Addison's time. Notices of this sort had been inserted in the very earliest newspapers, and were, no doubt, continued in the *Spectator* in deference to a popular demand. Advertisements often occupied as much as a column and a half of the paper. These advertisements are different from the business and professional announcements of to-day, and they reflect the manners and interests of the people as pointedly, if not so gracefully, as the discussions of the essayist himself. The following are facsimile reproductions from original numbers of the *Spectator* (1711):

Incomparable Perfuming Drops for Handkerchiefs, and all other Linnen Cloaths, Gloves, &c. being the moſt Excellent for that purpoſe in the Univerſe; for they Stain nothing that is perfumed with 'em, any more than fair Water, but are the moſt Deleƈtable, Fragrant, and Odoriferous Perfume in Nature, and good againſt all Diſeaſes of the Head and Brain: By their delicious Smell, they Comfort, Revive, and Refreſh all the Senſes, Natural, Vital and Animal, enliven the Spirits, chear the Heart, and drive away Melancholy: They alſo perfume Rooms, Beds, Preſſes, Drawers, Boxes, &c. making them ſmell ſurprizingly Fine and Odoriferous. They Perfume the Hands excellently, are an extraordinary Scent for the Pocket; and, in ſhort, are ſo exceeding Pleaſant and Delightful, ſo admirably Curious and Delicate. and of ſuch general Uſe, that nothing in the World can compare with 'em. Sold only at Mr. Payn's Toy ſhop, at the Angel and Crows. In St. Paul's Church-yard, near Cheapſide, at 2 s. 6 d. a Bottle, with Direƈtions.

At the Requeſt of ſeveral Foreigners lately arrived, The Maſquerade in Old Spring Garden, Charing Croſs, will be this preſent Tueſday, being the Firſt Day of May. Note, That upon this Occaſion a Gentleman is pleaſed to give for the Diverſion of the Maſquers, an Entertainment of Muſick, both Vocal and Inſtrumental, by ſome of the beſt Maſters in London. This Entertainment will begin exactly at Ten a Clock. Tickets may be had at Mr. Thurmonds's in King's Court, Ruſſel-ſtreet, Covent-Garden, and at the Houſe in Spring Garden; price Half a Guinea. No perſon whatſoever to be admitted Unmaſk'd or Arm'd.

INFLUENCE OF THE SPECTATOR.—The life of the people of England at the beginning of the eighteenth century finds full and vivid presentation in the *Spectator*. The volume of 635 papers offers in passing-show the men and women of both the upper and lower classes, displaying their fooleries and extravagances in dress, and their indulgence in many forms of sensual pleasures or in such grosser vices as gambling, dueling, ɔr playing the Mohock. As the Spectator observes, "there were both those who passed the time in crimes and immoralities and those who passed the time in trifle and impertinence." The diaries of a fine gentleman and of a fine lady are given in the *Spectator*. They show how utterly purposeless and debaséd were the lives of the dandy and the coquette. The dissection of a beau's head (No. 275) showed that the antra contained no sign of ideas, the cavities being filled with ribbons, billets-doux, snuff, and flatteries. In another paper (No. 10) we are told that these blanks of society "never know what to talk of till twelve o'clock in the morning, but by that time they are pretty good judges of the weather and know which way the wind sits." A survey of English history during the forty-two years preceding the accession of Queen Anne will do much toward accounting for the temperament and conduct of these people. They had found no time to consider the claims of culture amidst a long war with France, the development of strong party interests, and the phenomenal expansion of the nation's trade.

Beneath the corruption and frivolity of the people there was, however, a dormant sense of refinement. The earnestness and integrity of former generations had not been entirely rooted out. There came a time when two men, with kindly hearts and able minds, saw an opportunity for recalling the people to proper living and thinking. On March 1, 1711, the *Spectator* papers began to appear. The public were immediately captivated with their quaint humor and their clever exposure of shams. The popularity of these daily speculations is not overdrawn in the tribute of George Trusty (No. 134):

"The variety of your subject surprizes me as much as a box of pictures did formerly in which there was only one face, that by pulling some isinglass over it was changed into a grave senator or a merry Andrew, a patched lady or a nun, a beau or a black-a-moor, a prude or a coquett, a country squire or a conjurer, with many other different representations very entertaining tho' still the same at the bottom. This was a childish amusement when I was carried away with the outward appearance, but you make a deeper impression and affect the secret springs of the minds; you charm the fancy, soothe the passions, and insensibly lead the reader to that sweetness of temper that you so well describe; you rouse generosity with the spirit, and inculcate humanity with that ease that he must be miserably stupid that is not affected by

you. I can't say indeed that you have put impertinence to silence or
vanity out of countenance; but methinks you have bid as fair for it as
any man that ever appeared upon a public stage; and offer an infallible
cure of vice and folly for the price of one penny."

The influence exerted by Addison and Steele in these diurnal essays
brought health and vigor back again into English social life. The
Spectator became the mirror wherein men and women saw the folly and
absurdity of their conduct, yet without feeling the sting of malignant
caricature. Each issue of the folio sheet hastened the final reform by
its reinforcement of good taste, its incitement to higher purposes in life,
and its presentation of subjects more worthy to engage the discussion
of the gentlemen who lounged in the coffeehouses. Addison unques-
tionably realized the ambition which he confesses in No. 556,—"Not
to increase the number either of Whigs or Tories, but of wise and good
men."

THE SPECTATOR'S PLACE IN LITERATURE.—It is not their ethical
value, entirely, which has made Addison's essays popular for two hundred years. A permanent charm consists in their simplicity and refinement of diction. These qualities had not been combined in the prose of
earlier controversial literature and satire. But the eighteenth century
produced an author whose style possesses both elegance and ease. With
Addison there are no artifices of construction, no flashes of eloquence,
and yet, he is able to make an English sentence agreeable to the ear and,
at the same time, poignant in thought. All this may be said, recogniz-
ing meanwhile that Addison frequently violates the rules of modern
syntax and persistently ignores the principle of sentence coherence.
But the grace and delicacy of his expression are not destroyed by faulty
constructions. In reading the *De Coverley Papers* we discover that a
certain refinement in language is possible and natural, even in the treatment of familiar everyday topics. The style of these papers has been
called conversational. This being so, we who live in the present can
well make the dignity and purity of the Spectator's talk the touchstone
for our own speech.

Again, these essays on the "gentle art of living" owe much of their
charm to a narrative, and a distinctly human interest attached to the
fortunes and movements of that imaginary group of gentlemen who were
members of the Spectator Club. Sir Roger, reflecting the "unpretend-

ing virtues and amicable weaknesses" of a typical country gentleman, is the central figure. Next in prominence and in our affection is the Spectator himself—modest, courteous, and shrewd,—the quiet observer of men and the exact recorder of manners. Will Honeycomb, the man of fashion; Sir Andrew, the enterprising merchant; and the others in that immortal company, appear and reappear before us, until the drama is ended and the Spectator himself retires from the stage. Indeed, the charm of the *Spectator* essay will be felt just as long as there is a demand for a style combining purity and elegance with faithful portrayal of life and character.

SUGGESTIONS FOR STUDY

PRELIMINARY READING.—A knowledge of the historical setting of the *Spectator* papers seems indispensable. The teacher must be equipped with that broad background of knowledge which, as Professor Palmer explains, will enable one "to teach right up to the edge of his knowledge without a fear of falling off." This preparatory reading, besides being readily accessible, will clothe every page of the text with new meaning and interest. Only a few sources of information need be consulted. An excellent work is the *Life of Addison*, by William J. Courthope, in *English Men of Letters Series;* Chap. V., on the *Tatler* and the *Spectator*, will prove especially valuable. Other volumes to be consulted are John Ashton's *Social Life in the Reign of Queen Anne*, Green's *History of the English People*, and William C. Sydney's *England and the English in the Eighteenth Century*. Biographies of Addison and Steele, as well as criticisms of their works, are too well known to be mentioned here.

A very fruitful way of beginning the study of the *De Coverley Papers* is to assign various subjects to the members of the class for investigation and report. Papers may be written upon such matters as are treated in Chap. III., Vol. I., of Macaulay's *History of England*. The class ought to be familiar with Macaulay's interesting descriptions of The Country Gentleman, London, The Coffeehouses, Newspapers, et cetera.

NOTEBOOKS.—When the reading of the paper is taken up, notebooks may be used to great advantage. Each student should set down the following titles (allowing a page for each one) under which he will write

such data as he finds in the course of his reading:—(1) Traits of Sir
Roger; (2) Traits of the Spectator; (3) Life in the Country; (4) Life in
London; (5) Amusements; (6) Party Spirit,—and similar headings.
Other pages of the notebook may comprise a special dictionary. Here
will be kept a list of words—now obsolete or unfamiliar to the student—
with the meanings indicated by synonyms or brief explanatory notes.
The list would contain such terms as *coral* (p. 14, l. 14), *blots* (p. 16,
l. 19), *habits* (p. 23, l. 17), *mode* (p. 23, l. 19), *polite* (p. 27, l. 26), *pad*
(p. 30, l. 1), *conversation* (p. 30, l. 28), *humorist* (p. 30, l. 33), *husband*
(p. 34, l. 14), *event* (p. 52, l. 8), *murrain* (p. 52, l. 14), *vapors* (p. 61, l. 8),
freedoms (p. 82, l. 31), *put* (p. 144, l. 25), and especially "wit" and
"parts," which frequently appear.

The use of the notebook may be extended in various ways under
the direction of the teacher. An attractive and helpful department would
include a page or two of quotations selected by each student as examples
of the author's felicity in expression and excellence of sentiment.

ORAL RECITATION.—The class should not fail to recognize how
ingenious was the plan adopted by Steele and Addison in making Sir
Roger the central figure. A certain number of the thirty-three papers
have for their special object the presentation of the Knight's character.
We see him at home, at church, at the assizes, and in the city. While
always revealing his simplicity and innocence of mind, he betrays in
each new situation some curious whim or vanity. Many of the papers
describing the Spectator's visit to Coverley Hall contribute but little to
the presentation of Sir Roger's character. On the other hand, it is
because the Spectator is being entertained by the Knight that he finds
the opportunity of observing the habits and manners of the country
folk. Thus papers which only mention Sir Roger incidentally are concerned chiefly with the development of minor characters or with the
account of customs and beliefs which the author wishes to satirize in
other people. Again, there are several papers which are given over to
the reflections of the author upon some general topic and which contain
little or no account of persons. Therefore, one of the first points to be
discussed and determined is the purpose, or main idea, underlying each
separate paper.

Other important topics to be treated in the oral recitation are briefly
suggested in the following questions:

What types of character are reflected in the various persons mentioned in the papers?

How are the characteristics of each of these persons brought out,—by what he does or says, or by the author's comment?

Wherever satire appears explain exactly what is being satirized and how the author goes about it.

Give your own impression of Sir Andrew, Will Honeycomb, Tom Touchy, The Chaplain, Will Wimble.

Which author, Addison or Steele, puts the greater feeling into his writing?

Where in the papers does Addison show his Whig prejudices?

Are Addison's sentences loose or periodic in form?

Which of the following qualities of style are found to be most conspicuous in Addison's writing,—simplicity, strength, clearness, taste, melody, pathos, humor?

What evidences of Sir Roger's self-importance do you find in the papers?

Why was it necessary to have Sir Roger die?

Explain and discuss the principal allusions to city and country life.

CORRELATED READING IN THE SPECTATOR. Because the practice has always been found both enjoyable and profitable, it is well that the class should be required to read several numbers of the *Spectator* outside the De Coverley collection. Undoubtedly the best arrangement is to have the volumes of the *Spectator* papers upon the teacher's desk (the edition in *Everyman's Library*—4 volumes, introduction by Professor Gregory Smith—is inexpensive and especially good: the edition of Henry Morley is well known). At the close of as many recitations as practicable, the last five minutes may be devoted to this reading. An appropriate paper should be selected by the teacher and the book then passed to some member of the class who will read the selection aloud. On the following day the contents of the paper may be reviewed in a very brief discussion. The scope and attractiveness of the material to be found in the *Spectator* will at once become evident. A few instances are given here: *On Clubs*, No. 9; *On Purpose of the Spectator*, Nos. 10, 124, and 262; *Popularity of Puppet-Shows*, No. 14; *On Fashions in Head-Dress*, No. 98; *On Dress*, No. 129; *On Flirtations with a Fan*, No. 134; *On Low Standards of Theatre-Goers*, No. 208; *On Use of Mottoes*

and the Letters, No. 221; *The Cries of London,* No. 251; *On Sir Roger's
Popularity with the People,* No. 271; *The Dissection of a Coquett's Heart,*
No. 281; *Journal of a Gentleman,* No. 317; *Manifesto of the Mohocks,*
No. 347; *False Ambitions of Women,* No. 435; *On Behavior in Church,*
Nos. 460 and 630.

WRITTEN COMPOSITION.—No other classic in the list of required reading furnishes so many suggestions for the writing of themes. In the
case of the *De Coverley Papers* the usual objections to making literature
a basis for written composition are not sustained. Subjects may be
chosen which require invention as well as imitation, and which are
certain to enlist the student's interest. The following are given by way
of suggestion:

1. A Day's Fishing with Will Wimble.
2. Sir Roger and Will Honeycomb—compared.
3. A Letter from the Chaplain containing an Account of his Last
Visit and Talk with the Old Baronet.
4. Country Life in the Eighteenth Century.
5. The Spectator's Account of his Visit to the Pyramids.
6. Sir Roger while in London attends Church with the Spectator.
7. A Sketch of the Widow.
8. Addison's Skill in using Satire.
9. The Coffeehouses.
10. A paper in imitation of Nos. 120 and 121, in which the Spectator
discusses the instinct of some animals not mentioned in either of these
essays.
11. Sir Roger's Hunting Pack.
12. A Description of the real Moll White.
13. A History of the Suit,—Tom Touchy *vs.* Will Wimble.

QUESTIONS AND NOTES

(Figures in heavy type refer to page and line.)

THE SPECTATOR, PP. 13–18.—How does this paper secure the interest
of the public in subsequent numbers?

In what respects does the Spectator's description of himself conform
to the life and temperament of Addison?

Point out what is humorous and what is serious in the Spectator's account of himself.

Was Addison a Whig or a Tory?

The *Spectator* was published every week day from March 1, 1711, to December 6, 1712,—making 555 issues. The paper was revived January 18, 1714, and was published three times each week until December 20th of the same year.

Coffeehouses. 16 : 3. There are nineteen different coffeehouses mentioned in the *Spectator* papers. Additional comment upon the popularity of these resorts may be found in Chap. III, Vol. I, of Macaulay's *History of England* and in Chap. XVIII of Ashton's *Social Life in the Reign of Queen Anne.*

The papers written by Addison are signed C, L, I, and O, the idea being derived from the name of the Muse of History. Papers contributed by Steele are signed R and T. For a very interesting and entertaining discussion of the use of these letters, see *Spectator*, No. 221.

THE SPECTATOR CLUB, PP. 18–24.—What classes of society are represented in the Club?

What points concerning Sir Roger's character arouse the most interest?

What matter is given the most emphasis in the characterization of the Templar?

How is the ideal merchant reflected in Sir Andrew?

What is the purpose of including Will Honeycomb among the members of the Club? Is the Will Honeycomb type of man to be found in society to-day?

What is attractive in the personality of Captain Sentry?

SIR ROGER ON MEN OF FINE PARTS, PP. 25–28.—The aim of this paper is to urge the importance of making morality and religion the foundation for all true culture, or to show that sharpness of intellect and polish of manners are noxious affectations unless they grow out of nature and reason. Examine each paragraph to discover how this thought is developed or applied.

SIR ROGER AT HOME, PP. 29–32.—How is Sir Roger's character revealed in his home life?

What traits of country people are brought out in this paper?

Captain Sentry, after succeeding to Sir Roger's estate, makes mention of "his little absurdities and incapacity for the conversation of the politest men." What warrant do you find for Sentry's characterization in this account of Sir Roger?

How is the kindliness of Addison's humor reflected in this description of life at Coverley Hall?

SIR ROGER'S SERVANTS, PP. 32–36.—Is Sir Roger's policy as a master tempered with too much generosity?

What inconsistency is found in the statements of l. 5, p. 35, and l. 17, p. 29? Note the authors of the respective papers.

What reform has Steele in mind in this discussion?

SIR ROGER AND WILL WIMBLE, PP. 36–39.—Why is the letter extraordinary?

Look up the meaning of *Wimble* in an unabridged dictionary and show the appropriateness of the name.

How is all of Will Wimble's time employed?

What career does Addison recommend for the younger brothers in English families?

Read the author's comment upon crowded professions in *Spectator*, No. 21.

SIR ROGER'S ANCESTORS, PP. 39–43.—To what extent is Sir Roger's pride in his lineage justifiable?

What is Sir Roger's idea of a gentleman?

What was Sir Andrew's reason for claiming that the citizen and benefactor referred to by Sir Roger was a real ancestor of the Coverley family?

What is the purpose of the paper?

NIGHT FEARS AT COVERLEY, PP. 43–47.—What is Addison's own position in this matter of apparitions? Is he entirely free from superstition himself?

Does he accept the opinions of philosophers (and poets) in reference to ghosts?

What does he wish to correct in the belief of the country people?

Why does he introduce the story from Josephus?

A SUNDAY WITH SIR ROGER, PP. 47–50.—What special value belonging to a Sabbath in the country does the author wish the readers of the town to recognize?

What faults and what virtues of Sir Roger are revealed? Which predominate?

What objectionable features of church life in the country are exposed? What conditions prevailed in city congregations? See Nos. 460 and 630 of the *Spectator*.

Account for the universal interest and delight which is found in this paper.

SIR ROGER IN LOVE, PP. 50–55.—In what sense is the pleasing walk "settled upon" the widow?

How long a time has elapsed since Sir Roger became infatuated with his charming client?

How has the unsuccessful suit affected the life of the old squire? Has he lost any of his ardor for the widow?

What is the significance of Sir Roger's assertion that the widow is a "desperate scholar"?

Are Sir Roger's attainments superior to those of the average country gentleman of that time?

Compare Sir Roger with the typical country squire as he is described by Macaulay. (*History of England*, Chap. III.)

SIR ROGER'S ECONOMY, PP. 56–59.—Does the shame of poverty lead people of the present day to live in the absurd fashion adopted by Sir Roger's guest?

Did Steele in his own life practice the economy which he extols in this discussion?

What custom is Steele following in naming these imaginary persons *Laertes* and *Irus?*

BODILY EXERCISE, PP. 60–63.—What kind of recreation or exercise does Addison indorse?

Does he approve of Sir Roger's devotion to hunting?

Where do you find satire delicately employed in this discussion?

SIR ROGER AND THE CHASE, PP. 64–69.—Who is the author of this paper? Look up the facts of his life in Introduction, pp. 9–10. With what success has he imitated the style of Addison in this account of the chase?

In what respects does Sir Roger represent the typical country gentleman?

Does the Spectator display his usual manner and disposition on this occasion? Find the place in the account where he really speaks out.

How is this narrative of the hunt made vivid and entertaining?

What difference is to be noted in Sir Roger's spirit and conduct when hunting foxes and when hunting hares?

MOLL WHITE, THE WITCH, PP. 69–72.—The belief in witchcraft was very general in the last half of the seventeenth century. Less than twenty years before this paper was published the extensive panic over witchcraft occurred in Salem, Mass. The last witch's trial in England was that of Jane Wenham in 1712. The *Encyclopedia Britannica* gives some account of the famous trial of the Suffolk witches. These were two widows accused of bewitching young children. The evidence set forth that the children fell into fits and vomited crooked pins. A farmer testified that after his cart had touched the house of one of these witches it overturned continually and they could not get it home. The chief baron, summing up, said that there were such creatures as witches because the Scriptures affirmed it and the wisdom of nations had provided laws against such persons.

Is the author altogether incredulous on the subject of witchcraft? Compare his statement at the end of the first paragraph with his statement on p. 70, l. 11.

What is Sir Roger's opinion of Moll White?

What more does the author wish to accomplish besides correcting the injustice which attended the belief in witchcraft?

LOVE-MAKING AT COVERLEY, PP. 73–76.—What is the real theme of the author,—Sir Roger's admiration for the widow, or the impertinence of confidantes and busybodies, or the love-making of Sir Roger's Master of the Game?

To what cause does Steele attribute all of Sir Roger's eccentricities?

She. 76 : 1. To whom does the pronoun refer?

COUNTRY MANNERS, PP. 77–79.—What have the town and country to learn from each other in regard to etiquette?

Why are the manners and ceremonies of the city folk and country folk so unlike?

What different meanings has the term *conversation* in this paper?

In relation to headdresses (p. 79) be sure to read Nos. 98 and 265 of the *Spectator*.

SIR ROGER'S POULTRY, PP. 80–83, AND THE ADAPTATION OF ANIMALS, PP. 84–89.—These papers are in no way connected with the sketches of men and of manners that are included in this collection. But they are interesting inasmuch as they deal with pleasing topics of natural history and are examples of a great number of easy philosophical discussions which Addison contributed to the *Spectator*. The author's purpose is to show that the habits and instincts of animals demonstrate the existence of a Divine Energy acting in every creature.

SIR ROGER AMONG HIS NEIGHBORS, PP. 89–92.—What traits of Sir Roger are revealed in his criticism of Tom Touchy? By his Speech at Court?

What is the satire in the story of the Saracen's head?

What prompts the Spectator to word his reply to Sir Roger's question (p. 92, fourth line from end) as he does? See p. 91, l. 2.

THE STORY OF FLORIO AND LEONILLA, PP. 93–97.—Addison frequently introduced a fable or allegory in the *Spectator* papers to impress a matter of principle.

What do we learn concerning the education of a man of considerable estate?

What is the purpose of this discussion?

Like a novel. 94 : 9. What was understood by this term at that time?

PARTY SPIRIT, PP. 98–102, AND POLITICAL DISSENSIONS, PP. 102–106.—
The origin of the two parties, Whigs and Tories, dates back to the reign of Charles II. The first controversy involved the question of the hereditary rights of kings. Parliament in 1679 wished to prevent the succession to the throne of James of York, a Catholic and a brother of

Charles. Those who opposed the succession of James drafted what was known as the Exclusion Bill. The king, to save his brother, dissolved Parliament. The members who aimed to pass the bill and therefore petitioned Charles to summon Parliament again, were called Petitioners, or Whigs; while those who sustained Charles were known as Abhorrers, or Tories. Thus, the first great principle advocated by the Whigs was the right of the people to create kings and to limit their exercise of power. The Tories supported the theory of the Divine Right of Kings as well as their absolute authority in government.

James II, who succeeded his brother Charles, inflamed the people by his efforts to restore Catholicism. When finally he fled to France and William and Mary became the sovereigns, Parliament quickly passed the Toleration Act which gave to the Dissenters (Presbyterians, Independents, Quakers) the privilege of worshiping according to their own beliefs. The Tories hated the Catholics as bitterly as did the Whigs. Consequently, there was little opposition to such a movement, because the Tories, while they still believed in the Anglican Church, were willing to accept the Act so long as it excluded Catholics from its benefits. In succeeding years, however, the jealousy of the English Church Advocates increased and they stoutly opposed the freedom of the Nonconformists. The Tories constituted the Church Party and the Whigs were in sympathy with the Dissenters.

The reference to the opposition between the landed and the moneyed interests (p. 104, l. 23) was a still later development of party differences. The expansion of trade referred to in the foregoing notes (p. 151) is apparent in the spread of manufactures throughout the English cities. Merchants were becoming wealthy by means of increased exports. This gave origin to the strife between country gentlemen, whose land taxes were very heavy, and merchants who only paid small excise duties. The country districts were the strongholds of the Tories and the cities of the Whigs.

Sum up the objections which the Spectator makes against partisanship.

Why does Sir Roger say that parties tend to the destruction of the game? (p. 99, l. 2).

Does this description of the evils of party spirit apply to conditions to-day in England? *Spectator*, No. 451, discusses the evils of supporting one's party with falsehood and slander.

SIR ROGER AND THE GYPSIES, PP. 106–109.—Is entertainment or instruction the chief aim of this paper?

How do Sir Roger's actions contradict his words?

What evidence is there that the Spectator was a close observer of human nature?

THE SPECTATOR SUMMONED TO LONDON, PP. 109–112.—What figure is effectively employed in the second paragraph?

What is the special purpose of the paper?

What is attractive in Will Honeycomb's letter?

How does it reflect the interest which the papers have aroused among town readers?

White witch. 111 : 3. One who could undo the wrong or evil spells of the black spirits and who yet indulged in certain mischief.

THE JOURNEY TO LONDON, PP. 112–116.—What information is given concerning the usual experiences to be encountered in traveling by coach at the beginning of the eighteenth century?

What new types of people are presented and satirized in this paper?

A DEBATE AT THE CLUB, PP. 116–120.—What is the precise reproach that Sir Roger casts upon the trading class?

What virtue of the country gentleman does Sir Roger extol in contrast with the merchant's frugality?

What claims does Sir Andrew make concerning the usefulness of merchantmen?

How does Sir Andrew show the real worth of him who only "pores over cashbooks and exercises skill in numbers."

How does Sir Andrew finally silence Sir Roger by reminding him of the obligation of his family to a certain man of trade? See **120 : 7** and **42 : 13–19.**

Who has the better of the argument?

Does Steele seem to be giving little or great credit to Sir Andrew? Why?

SIR ROGER IN LONDON, PP. 120–124.—What new impression do we get of the old baronet?

What is Addison's reason for having Sir Roger come to town? His purpose in having him tell about Will Wimble, Moll White, and Tom Touchy?

Discuss the appropriateness of the Latin motto for this paper.

Examine the division of the paper into paragraphs, and tell whether or not each paragraph develops a new topic.

SIR ROGER IN WESTMINSTER ABBEY, PP. 125–130.—What is the point of Addison's satire in mentioning Sir Roger's frequent citation of Baker's *Chronicle?*

Point out other weaknesses of Sir Roger that are satirized in this account.

What is at the bottom of the Knight's admiration for the various persons whose tombs were inspected?

How does he betray his political prejudice?

SIR ROGER AND BEARDS, PP. 130–134.—This paper was written chiefly for the purpose of entertainment. The discussion, however, may be seriously applied in a few instances to frivolities of the time. What would likely be the moral which the Spectator promises in another paper?

SIR ROGER AT THE PLAY, PP. 134–138.—Why was *The Committee* a play which would please Sir Roger?

Look up the account of the barbarities committed by the Mohocks (*Spectator*, Nos. 324 and 347).

How are we impressed by the account of the special attention paid Sir Roger by his friends who escort him to and from the theater?

Account for the behavior of Sir Roger at the play.

What mental capacity of Sir Roger is reflected in his comments upon the action and the characters of the play?

The Distressed Mother, 134: **Note 2.** A criticism of this play appears in the *Spectator*, No. 338, and is answered in No. 341. See also No. 290. The prologue of the play was written by Steele and the epilogue by Addison.

WILL HONEYCOMB AT THE CLUB, PP. 139–142.—Compare the two lovers,—Sir Roger and Will Honeycomb.

What class of men is typified in Will Honeycomb?

Do his experiences seem probable?

Do we have an utter contempt for him?

Other interesting accounts of Will Honeycomb may be found in *Spectator*, Nos. 105 and 499. No. 530 tells of Will's marriage.

SIR ROGER AT SPRING GARDEN, PP. 142–145.—How do the various incidents reported in this paper show the wide dissemblance in city and country manners?

What attractive qualities does Sir Roger exhibit?

What does the paper contribute toward the general purpose of the *Spectator?*

The following paragraph has been omitted from the text: "As we were going out of the garden, my old friend, thinking himself obliged as a member of the quorum to animadvert upon the morals of the place, told the mistress of the house, who sat at the bar, that he should be a better customer to her garden if there were more nightingales and fewer strumpets."

SIR ROGER'S DEATH, PP. 146–148.—What is the reason for having the particulars concerning Sir Roger's death, his funeral, and his will given in a letter from the butler?

What traits does Addison wish to be most prominent in our final estimate of Sir Roger?

Taking the papers in this collection as a whole how may we justify the statement of Macaulay that "Addison is entitled to be considered as the forerunner of the great English novelists"?

Find allusions in various papers to prove that the writer *was* a spectator—not a talker.

No. 544 (*Spectator*) contains a letter from Captain Sentry which gives the account of his coming to the succession of Sir Roger's estate and of his carrying out his old master's wishes.

Thus far we have seen that the author has concluded his sketches of three members of the club. Sir Roger has died. Will Honeycomb has been transformed from the rake to the sober husband of a plain country girl. Captain Sentry is living quietly upon the De Coverley estate.

It is interesting to know how the author disposes of the three remaining members of the club. The information is to be found in the following numbers of the *Spectator:* No. 541 tells us that the Templar has determined to lay aside his poetical studies in order to follow a closer pursuit of the law, and has put together, as a farewell essay, "*Some Thoughts Concerning Pronunciation and Action.*" In No. 549 we learn that Sir Andrew has retired from business and has purchased a great tract of land where he intends to provide work for a great many indigent persons. In the same paper the death of the clergyman is reported.

LITERARY CRITICISMS.

"But it is not for his reputation as the great author of 'Cato' and the 'Campaign,' or for his merits as Secretary of State, or for his rank and high distinction as My Lady Warwick's husband, or for his eminence as an Examiner of political questions on the Whig side, or a Guardian of British liberties, that we admire Joseph Addison. It is as a Tatler of small talk and a Spectator of mankind, that we cherish and love him, and owe as much pleasure to him as to any human being that ever wrote. He came in that artificial age, and began to speak with his noble, natural voice. He came, the gentle satirist, who hit no unfair blow; the kind judge, who castigated only in smiling. While Swift went about, hanging and ruthless—a literary Jeffries—in Addison's kind court only minor cases were tried: only peccadilloes and small sins against society: only a dangerous libertinism in tuckers and hoops; or a nuisance in the abuse of beaux' canes and snuff-boxes. It may be a lady is tried for breaking the peace of our sovereign lady Queen Anne, and ogling too dangerous from the side box: or a Templar for beating the watch, or breaking Priscian's head: or a citizen's wife for caring too much for the puppet-show, and too little for her husband and children: every one of the little sinners brought before him is amusing, and he dismisses each with the pleasantest penalties and the most charming words of admonition. . . . What would Sir Roger De Coverley be without his follies and his charming little brain-cracks? If the good knight did not call out to the people sleeping in church, and say 'Amen' with such a delightful pomposity: if he did not make a speech in the assize-court *apropos de bottes*, and merely to show his dignity to Mr. Spectator: if he did not mistake Madam Doll Tearsheet for a lady of quality in Temple Garden: if he were wiser than he is: if he had not his humor to salt his life, and were but a mere English gentleman and game-preserver—of what worth were he to us? We love him for his vanities as much as his virtues. What is ridiculous is delightful in him: we are so fond of him because we laugh at him so. And out of that laughter, out of those harmless eccentricities and follies, out of that touched brain, and out of that honest manhood and simplicity—we get a result of happiness, goodness, tenderness, pity, piety."—From Thackeray's *English Humorists*.

"He had read with critical eyes the important volume of human life, and knew the heart of man from the depths of stratagem to the surface of affectation. . . . He has restored virtue to its dignity, and taught innocence not to be ashamed. No greater felicity can genius attain than that of having purified intellectual pleasures, separated mirth from indecency, and wit from licentiousness; of having taught a succession of writers to bring elegance and gayety to the aid of goodness; and, if I may use expressions yet more awful, of having 'turned many to righteousness.' . . . His prose is the model of the middle style; on grave subjects not formal, on light occasions not groveling; pure without scrupulosity, and exact without apparent elaboration; always equable, and always easy, without glowing words or pointed sentences. . . . It was apparently his principal endeavor to avoid all harshness and severity of diction; he is therefore sometimes verbose in his transitions and connections, and sometimes descends too much to the language of conversation: yet if his language had been less idiomatical it might have lost somewhat of its genuine Anglicism. What he attempted he performed; he is never feeble, and he did not wish to be energetic; he is never rapid and he never stagnates. His sentences have neither studied amplitude, nor affected brevity; his periods, though not diligently rounded, are voluble and easy. Whoever wishes to attain an English style, familiar but not coarse, and elegant but not ostentatious, must give his days and nights to the volumes of Addison."—From Johnson's *Lives of the Poets*.

ECLECTIC ENGLISH CLASSICS

New Edition in Cloth. The 20 Cent Series

53 Volumes, including the following:

Addison's Sir Roger de Coverley Papers (Underwood) . .	$0.20
Arnold's Sohrab and Rustum (Tanner)	.20
Burke's Conciliation with the American Colonies (Clark) .	.20
Byron's Childe Harold (Canto IV), Prisoner of Chillon, Mazeppa, and other Selections (Venable)	.20
Carlyle's Essay on Burns (Miller)	20
Coleridge's Ancient Mariner (Garrigues)	.20
Defoe's Robinson Crusoe (Stephens)	.20
Dickens's Tale of Two Cities (Pearce). Double number .	.40
Franklin's Autobiography (Reid)	.20
George Eliot's Silas Marner (McKitrick)	.20
Goldsmith's Vicar of Wakefield (Hansen)	.20
Gray's Elegy in a Country Churchyard, and Goldsmith's Deserted Village (Van Dyke)	.20
Irving's Sketch Book — Selections (St. John)	.20
Lincoln, Selections from	.20
Macaulay's Essays on Lord Clive and Warren Hastings (Holmes) Double number	.40
Lays of Ancient Rome (Atkinson)	.20
Life of Johnson (Lucas)	.20
Milton's Minor Poems (Buck)	.20
Old Testament Narratives (Baldwin)	.20
Pope's Rape of the Lock, and Essay on Man (Van Dyke) .	.20
Scott's Ivanhoe (Schreiber). Double number	.40
Lady of the Lake (Bacon)	.20
Quentin Durward (Norris). Double number	.40
Shakespeare's As You Like It (North)	.20
Julius Caesar (Baker)	.20
Macbeth (Livengood)	.20
Merchant of Venice (Blakely)	.20
Midsummer-Night's Dream (Haney)	.20
Twelfth Night (Weld)	.20
Stevenson's Treasure Island (Fairley)	.20
Tennyson's Idylls of the King. Selections (Willard) . . .	.20
Princess (Shryock)	.20
Thackeray's Henry Esmond (Bissell). Triple number . .	.60
Washington's Farewell Address, and Webster's First Bunker Hill Oration (Lewis)	.20

AMERICAN BOOK COMPANY

(S.95)

A HISTORY OF ENGLISH LITERATURE

By REUBEN POST HALLECK, M.A. (Yale),
Louisville Male High School.   Price, $1.25

HALLECK'S HISTORY OF ENGLISH LITERATURE traces the development of that literature from the earliest times to the present in a concise, interesting, and stimulating manner. Although the subject is presented so clearly that it can be readily comprehended by high school pupils, the treatment is sufficiently philosophic and suggestive for any student beginning the study.

¶ The book is a history of literature, and not a mere collection of biographical sketches. Only enough of the facts of an author's life are given to make students interested in him as a personality, and to show how his environment affected his work. Each author's productions, their relations to the age, and the reasons why they hold a position in literature, receive adequate treatment.

¶ One of the most striking features of the work consists in the way in which literary movements are clearly outlined at the beginning of each chapter. Special attention is given to the essential qualities which differentiate one period from another, and to the animating spirit of each age. The author shows that each period has contributed something definite to the literature of England.

¶ At the end of each chapter a carefully prepared list of books is given to direct the student in studying the original works of the authors treated. He is told not only what to read, but also where to find it at the least cost. The book contains a special literary map of England in colors.

AMERICAN   BOOK   COMPANY
(S. 90)

A HISTORY OF AMERICAN
LITERATURE

By REUBEN POST HALLECK, M.A.,
Principal, Male High School, Louisville, Ky.

$1.25

A COMPANION volume to the author's History of
English Literature. It describes the greatest achievements in American literature from colonial times to
the present, placing emphasis not only upon men, but also
upon literary movements, the causes of which are thoroughly investigated. Further, the relation of each period
of American literature to the corresponding epoch of
English literature has been carefully brought out—and
each period is illuminated by a brief survey of its history.
¶ The seven chapters of the book treat in succession
of Colonial Literature, The Emergence of a Nation
(1754-1809), the New York Group, The New England
Group, Southern Literature, Western Literature, and the
Eastern Realists. To these are added a supplementary
list of less important authors and their chief works, as well
as A Glance Backward, which emphasizes in brief compass
the most important truths taught by American literature.
¶ At the end of each chapter is a summary which helps
to fix the period in mind by briefly reviewing the most significant achievements. This is followed by extensive historical and literary references for further study, by a very
helpful list of suggested readings, and by questions and
suggestions, designed to stimulate the student's interest and
enthusiasm, and to lead him to study and investigate further for himself the remarkable literary record of American
aspiration and accomplishment.

AMERICAN BOOK COMPANY

(S.318)

COMPOSITION-RHETORIC

By STRATTON D. BROOKS, Superintendent of
Schools, Boston, Mass., and MARIETTA HUB-
BARD, formerly English Department, High School,
La Salle, Ill.   Price, $1.00

THE fundamental aim of this volume is to enable pupils
to express their thoughts freely, clearly, and forcibly.
At the same time it is designed to cultivate literary
appreciation, and to develop some knowledge of rhetorical
theory.   The work follows closely the requirements of the
College Entrance Examination Board, and of the New
York State Education Department.

¶ In Part One are given the elements of description, narra-
tion, exposition, and argument; also special chapters on let-
ter-writing and poetry. A more complete and comprehensive
treatment of the four forms of discourse already discussed is
furnished in Part Two.   In each part is presented a series of
themes covering these subjects, the purpose being to give the
pupil inspiration, and that confidence in himself which comes
from the frequent repetition of an act.   A single new principle is introduced into each theme, and this is developed in
the text, and illustrated by carefully selected examples.

¶ The pupils are taught how to correct their own errors,
and also how to get the main thought in preparing their
lessons.   Careful coördination with the study of literature
and with other school studies is made throughout the book.

¶ The modern character of the illustrative extracts can not
fail to interest every boy and girl.   Concise summaries are
given following the treatment of the various forms of discourse,
and toward the end of the book there is a very comprehensive
and compact summary of grammatical principles. More than
usual attention is devoted to the treatment of argument.

AMERICAN BOOK COMPANY
(S. 88)

A PUNCTUATION PRIMER

By FRANCES M. PERRY, Associate Professor of Rhetoric and Composition, Wellesley College.

$0.30

THE Punctuation Primer is a manual of first principles or essentials simply and systematically presented; it is not an elaborate treatise on punctuation. It offers a few fundamental principles that are flexible and comprehensive, and easily understood and remembered. The meaning of the text to be punctuated and the grammatical structure of the sentence are made the bases for generalization and division.

¶ The discussion is taken up under two main divisions: The terminal punctuation of sentences, and the punctuation of elements within sentences. Under punctuation of elements within sentences, the punctuation of principal elements, of dependent elements, of coördinate elements, of independent elements, and of implied elements are considered in the order given.

¶ In addition, several important related topics are treated, such as paragraphing, quotations, capitalization, compound words, word divisions, the uses of the apostrophe, the preparation and the correction of manuscript, conventional forms for letters, the use of authorities in writing themes, the correction of themes, and the making of bibliographies.

¶ Throughout the carefully selected examples make clear the meaning of the text, while the exercises provided at each stage of the work afford the student practice in the correct application of the principles.

¶ Though written primarily to meet the needs of college freshmen, the primer is an excellent manual for high schools.

AMERICAN BOOK COMPANY
(S.84)

THE MASTERY OF BOOKS

By HARRY LYMAN KOOPMAN, A.M., Librarian
of Brown University.   Price, 90 cents

IN this book Mr. Koopman, whose experience and
reputation as a librarian give him unusual qualifications
as an adviser, presents to the student at the outset the
advantages of reading, and the great field of literature
open to the reader's choice.   He takes counsel with the
student as to his purpose, capacities, and opportunities in
reading, and aims to assist him in following such methods
and in turning to such classes of books as will further the
attainment of his object.

¶ Pains are taken to provide the young student from the
beginning with a knowledge, often lacking in older readers,
of the simplest literary tools—reference books and cata-
logues.   An entire chapter is given to the discussion of
the nature and value of that form of printed matter which
forms the chief reading of the modern world—periodical
literature.   Methods of note-taking and of mnemonics
are fully described ; and a highly suggestive and valuable
chapter is devoted to language study.

¶ One of the most valuable chapters in the volume to
most readers is that concerning courses of reading.   In
accordance with the author's new plan for the guidance
of readers, a classified list of about fifteen hundred books
is given, comprising the most valuable works in reference
books, periodicals, philosophy, religion, mythology and
folk-lore, biography, history, travels, sociology, natural
sciences, art, poetry, fiction, Greek, Latin, and modern
literatures.   The latest and best editions are specified, and
the relative value of the several works mentioned is indicated in notes.

AMERICAN BOOK COMPANY
(S. 106)

ESSENTIALS IN HISTORY

ESSENTIALS IN ANCIENT HISTORY . $1.50
From the earliest records to Charlemagne. By
ARTHUR MAYER WOLFSON, Ph.D., First
Assistant in History, DeWitt Clinton High School,
New York

**ESSENTIALS IN MEDIÆVAL AND MODERN
HISTORY** $1.50
From Charlemagne to the present day. By SAMUEL
BANNISTER HARDING, Ph.D., Professor of
European History, Indiana University

ESSENTIALS IN ENGLISH HISTORY . $1.50
From the earliest records to the present day. By
ALBERT PERRY WALKER, A.M., Master in
History, English High School, Boston

ESSENTIALS IN AMERICAN HISTORY. $1.50
From the discovery to the present day. By ALBERT
BUSHNELL HART, LL.D., Professor of History,
Harvard University

THESE volumes correspond to the four subdivisions
required by the College Entrance Examination
Board, and by the New York State Education Department. Each volume is designed for one year's work.
Each of the writers is a trained historical scholar, familiar
with the conditions and needs of secondary schools.

¶ The effort has been to deal only with the things which
are typical and characteristic; to avoid names and details
which have small significance, in order to deal more justly
with the forces which have really directed and governed
mankind. Especial attention is paid to social history.

¶ The books are readable and teachable, and furnish brief
but useful sets of bibliographies and suggestive questions.
No pains have been spared by maps and pictures to furnish
a significant and thorough body of illustration.

AMERICAN BOOK COMPANY
(S. 130)

DESCRIPTIVE CATALOGUE OF HIGH SCHOOL AND COLLEGE TEXTBOOKS

Published Complete and in Sections

WE issue a Catalogue of High School and College Textbooks, which we have tried to make as valuable and as useful to teachers as possible. In this catalogue are set forth briefly and clearly the scope and leading characteristics of each of our best textbooks. In most cases there are also given testimonials from well-known teachers, which have been selected quite as much for their descriptive qualities as for their value as commendations.

¶ For the convenience of teachers this Catalogue is also published in separate sections treating of the various branches of study. These pamphlets are entitled: English, Mathematics, History and Political Science, Science, Modern Foreign Languages, Ancient Languages, Commercial Subjects and Philosophy and Education. A separate pamphlet is devoted to the Newest Books in all subjects.

¶ Teachers seeking the newest and best books for their classes are invited to send for any of these.

¶ Copies of our price lists, or of special circulars, in which these books are described at greater length than the space limitations of the catalogue permit, will be mailed to any address on request. Address all correspondence to the nearest office of the company.

AMERICAN BOOK COMPANY
(S.312)